PART-TIME INCOME ENTERPRISE

Praise For

PART-TIME INCOME ENTERPRISE

"Jerry Scchittano has a map for you. It leads from this page to your bank account. Don't lose it. Don't ignore it. Just follow it to your dreams and watch them all come true. This wonderful book can transform those dreams into reality. It's not easy, but it sure is possible. I would wish you luck, but you won't need luck if you read this book."

—Jay Conrad Levinson

"Jerry has the unique ability to teach a proven moneymaking system while motivating the student to take action. The example's he uses makes it very easy to understand."

—Gary, Newport News, VA

"The forms for self evaluation and action taking are worth 10 times the cost of this book."

—Patsy Lee, Bentleyville, PA

"Reading this book is in itself a transforming experience. You get inside the minds of everyday people who took action and became entrepreneurial thinkers. Jerry lets you see how you can take action and create wealth"

—Michael, Jacksonville, FL

"*Part-Time Income Enterprise* is an easy to follow blueprint that if followed will change your life"

—Scott, Steam Boat Springs, CO

"A powerful program for anyone who is serious about earning extra income this information will work for people of all age's teenagers to retirees."

—**Lynn**, San Diego, CA

"So many books promise you pie in the sky hard to understand information. Jerry gets you in and gets you out with plain easy to understand strategies using real examples that keep you interested throughout the book."

—**Doris**, Morgantown, WVA

"If nothing else this book will give you the kick in the butt you need to get you from in front of the TV and start you thinking about how you can satisfy your needs and the needs of your family."

—**Justice**, 2ndLt., U.S.Army

"This is a great look at how normal ordinary every day people no matter where you live can make extra money. If you can't get excited about making extra money after reading this book, you need to check your pulse! Your Dead."

—**Marinka**, Holland

PART-TIME INCOME ENTERPRISE

*Your Road Map to Make Full-Time
Income With Part-Time Efforts*

JERRY SCICCHITANO

NEW YORK

PART-TIME INCOME ENTERPRISE
Your Road Map to Make Full-Time Income With Part-Time Efforts

Disclaimer: The Publisher and the Author make no representations or warranties with respect to the accuracy or completeness of the contents of this work and specifically disclaim all warranties, including without limitation warranties of fitness for a particular purpose. No warranty may be created or extended by sales or promotional materials. The advice and strategies contained herein may not be suitable for every situation. This work is sold with the understanding that the Publisher is not engaged in rendering legal, accounting, or other professional services. If professional assistance is required, the services of a competent professional person should be sought. Neither the Publisher nor the Author shall be liable for damages arising herefrom. The fact that an organization or website is referred to in this work as a citation and/or a potential source of further information does not mean that the Author or the Publisher endorses the information the organization or website may provide or recommendations it may make. Further, readers should be aware that internet websites listed in this work may have changed or disappeared between when this work was written and when it is read.

Before embarking on a part-time, income-producing venture, look at your lifestyle and realize that what others have accomplished is no indication of what you will accomplish. You will need to be committed to creating your part-time income venture, and please be realistic about how much time you are willing to devote to your part-time venture.

ISBN 978-1-61448-363-2 paperback
ISBN 978-1-61448-364-9 eBook
Library of Congress Control Number: 2012946014

Morgan James Publishing
The Entrepreneurial Publisher
5 Penn Plaza, 23rd Floor
New York City, New York 10001
(212) 655-5470 office • (516) 908-4496 fax
www.MorganJamesPublishing.com

Cover Design by:
Rachel Lopez
www.r2cdesign.com

Interior Design by:
Bonnie Bushman
bonnie@caboodlegraphics.com

In an effort to support local communities, raise awareness and funds, Morgan James Publishing donates a percentage of all book sales for the life of each book to Habitat for Humanity Peninsula and Greater Williamsburg.

Get involved today, visit
www.MorganJamesBuilds.com.

Habitat
for Humanity®
Peninsula and
Greater Williamsburg
Building Partner

**Our goal at Part-Time Income Enterprise is simple:
To help you reach yours.**

What appears to be the end may really be a new beginning.

As Will Rodgers said, "Even if you're on the right track, you'll get run over if you just sit there." **So let's get moving!**

TABLE OF CONTENTS

The standard table of contents you are used to finding in the front of most books will not be found here. In "Part-Time Income Enterprise" the organization (format of this book) was developed to allow for the presentation of one principal at a time with more advanced principles being reached only after basic understandings have been established. I am convinced that this step-by-step development of subject matter, simple discussion, and generous practice will enable you to progress faster than even you thought possible.

The business profiles are not going to be arranged by categories, because I want to keep your thought process open. While reading one opportunity, you may be able to group its concept with another and come up with your own enterprise concept.

Always be true to your dreams, and keep them alive. Never let anyone change your mind about what you feel you can achieve. Always believe in yourself.

Come along with us now and you will see what we mean while meeting some real life, rather unusual teachers.

PREFACE

Dear Reader of *Part-Time Income Enterprise:*

For the past several years, through my writings and seminars, I've taught hundreds of people how to achieve financial freedom through their own part-time, income-producing enterprise.

Now it's your turn.

IF YOU CAN'T FIND A WAY TO FOCUS YOUR EFFORTS, YOU WILL NOT MAKE ANY MONEY IN YOUR PART-TIME INCOME ENTERPRISE

In these pages, I'm going to show you how to get yourself focused and save yourself time and provide you an easy-to-follow plan to reach your extra income goal.

Believe me; I've been making part-time income for years now. When I first got into the part-time-income field, I couldn't get focused. I listened to this guy, that guy, another guy, every guy, and I got information overload and didn't take action.

I wasn't able to pick a project and stay focused and finish it. I would read a book or part of a book, or take some information from someone and try to put that information to use to make money for myself.

Some of the books had great information, and I thought I could make money from that information. I would start that project. The problem was that I would never finish it.

I was always searching for something better. I was always looking for the next big thing. I was looking for something that didn't exist. I was looking for something that didn't require much work and was going to make me a millionaire overnight.

There is no product that is going to do that for you!

I had the information in my hands to make a handsome living. I just wasn't using it. I wasn't staying focused on a project long enough to see any returns.

I was lied to, like most people who get into the money-making field. We are told by people who want to sell their products to us that we will make a million dollars overnight and don't have to do much work.

Guess what, you won't make that kind of money overnight, and it does take some work. What you should do is pick some projects and finish them. Once you start finishing your projects, whatever they may be, whether it's creating a product, building a website, starting a lawn service business, etc., the money will start coming in.

I always say that the toughest dollar to make is the first one. There are so many people that don't make any money and give up and go back to their day jobs. The first dollar was definitely the toughest for me to make. I think it gets easier because, once you have made some money, you have broken down that first very important barrier, and then it gets a lot easier.

You realize that you really can make that extra part-time income and your confidence soars! You can just keep on doing what you were doing to make more money. Work harder and expand your business. Repeat what you're doing to make money, just keep expanding on that process, and keep working on ways to improve your business.

Focus and hard work is going to get you a long way in life. Using focus and hard work to make money are two major keys to success. Don't let anyone else tell you otherwise.

What will all of this get for you? A lifestyle that gives you the freedom to do what you want, when you want, with whomever you want.

Prosperously yours,

Jerry Scicchitano

PS: The Buck Starts Here

ACKNOWLEDGMENTS

This book is dedicated to my family, for their encouragement and support. The Morgan James publishing team for their guidance, and all the entrepreneurs referenced in this book who shared their stories.

Brad Jessie William Kreg Margo Herb Ernie Katrina & Jen Ilene & Bonnie Marvin Margaret Elizabeth Brandon Jim & Josh Phil Tim Kelly Kimberly Vincent Trey Jan Chuck Linda & Margo Craig Jeremy Caron Mark Sheila Elona Calvin Sam & Molly Judy Rita Dannie Karen Patricia Amy Jeremy Jane Guy Steve George Susan & Robert Big G Patsy Lee Adrienne Terry Edward Sophie Paul Sonya Tom & Joann Christina Calvina Bruce Mason JoJo Gram Stan Ski Billy Kari & John Richard James Aaron Phil Adam Regina Brian & Mary Jo Erica Ronda Don Jan & Sharon Bobby Edward Patsy Sandy Clint David Bagley Ken Diane Jeff John Bill Dan Dave & Philip Shaun Justice Mark Emily Frank Ike E-Juror #3 Angela Amy Mike Debra Todd Beth Kim Smitty Janice

WELCOME TO
THE FIRST DAY OF
THE REST OF YOUR LIFE

This book is designed specifically for those of you who want to improve your present financial position.

- It will motivate you to take the first step along the way to certain success.
- It will show you how to discover your own money-earning potential and to put it to work for your special benefit.

You will learn numerous ways to turn your everyday activities into money-earning operations, with little extra effort on your part!

These result-producing, step-by-step instructions will take you all the way from the park bench to Park Avenue.

Let's be honest:

You bought this book for one, or both, of these two reasons:

1. You're looking for more money. You want some extra income, and you want it quick!
- You're looking for a challenge and want to try a part-time enterprise that could buy your freedom from the time clock.

PLEASE REMEMBER, EXTRA INCOME ENTERPRISE IS ABOUT **YOU...YOUR LIFE...YOUR FAMILY...YOUR FUTURE...YOUR GOALS**

Life certainly is different here at *Part-Time Income Enterprise* in a good way!

When your...wife...husband...mother...father...neighbor...friend tells you that *you cannot, will not, shall not,* ever make enough extra income to pay the bills or provide all the extras for your family with just the skills you have, what do you do?

When they say that your idea is

- dumb
- stupid
- idiotic

When they say that you don't have what it takes, you never worked for yourself...

What do you say?

And when they tell you that people won't pay for what you have to offer...

What do you say?

More to the point...

When they're trying *desperately* to *drag you* down into the same muck and mire of failed dreams and lost hope that they're in...

What do you do?

Here's what I do:

I smile politely and back away, because both they and their words are *poison* to my success. Making a full-time living—and even an insane fortune—is entirely possible, and you and I *know this* for a *fact*. I do it and did it for years. There are new people doing it every single day of the week. And if *they* can do it, *you* can do it.

Let me say that again...If *they* can do it, *you* can do it.

Because the only difference between the people who have made it and those who haven't made it, is that those who made it took serious *action*.

This is the *only, only, only* difference!

Take total, complete, full-steam-ahead *action*. Now, certainly there are many ways to make extra income. The method I chose was to get the very best tools and training possible. This book will enable you to save yourself time and provide you an easy-to-follow plan to reach your extra income goal.

But the point is, I never ever let those naysayers (and I've known plenty) drag me down into their dismal world. If they want to work 9 to 5 for the rest of their lives for someone else, so be it. But you and I want *more*. We want *better*. We want to be in control of when and where we work and what we do. **It's called *Freedom*.**

The freedom to *choose* the life we want to lead.

So when those naysayers tell you why you will never make enough extra income that you need to earn, so you can provide the extras for your family and yourself...just smile and back away. Do *not* tell them about how you are going to do it, just work your plan. Let it be a complete *secret* that you are quickly and quietly building your own part-time empire with the help and guidance of already successful part-time income builders. Let it be a complete secret to your friends and family that you are watching your income go from

- a couple of hundred the first month
- to several hundred the second month
- to several *thousand* a few months after that

Here's the link to my site, **www.parttimeincomeenterprise. com**, where you can sign up for my free blog.

 Scan this barcode with your
smart phone and it will
take you to my web site
www.parttimeincomeenterprise.com

This book will provide the help and guidance you need, because you are *not* a naysayer, because you are *ready* to make a stand for yourself, and because you're ready to get the life and freedom you've been craving for years. Welcome to a world where anything is possible, a world where you *can* and *will* build your part-time business faster than *even you* thought possible.

P.S. *"When people warn me against doing something, once my mind is made up, I grow increasingly determined to try it."*

—*Richard Branson*

Sound advice from one of the richest, self-made businessmen in the world, who, by the way, is a naysayer to *nothing:*

Part-Time Income Enterprise **Will Help**
You Achieve Top Extra Income

Today, many people are looking for additional income to handle the constantly rising cost of living. For several years, I have worked successfully at improving my own income. Moving into a better-paying position is one way to increase the money flow, but it has its limitations. You can go only so far, and you are always at the mercy of those above you.

In recent years, I have concentrated on developing and producing "extra income" money. This is a rewarding activity, not only financially, but also in self-satisfaction. It offers me hope of an even brighter future ahead, since extra income activities frequently become highly profitable full-time businesses.

Part-Time Income Enterprise will help you find the kind of extra income activity that is right for you. It will show you how you can turn this activity into big profits by working only a few extra hours a week.

Due to the stagnant business economy, many people who have jobs have their incomes leveling off, while their bills keep growing. Even people who make a top salary enjoy the freedom and excitement of earning an extra part-time income. Wouldn't it be nice to take that Caribbean cruise this year, rather than just driving to the beach? It is time you take control of your financial destiny. Work as much or as little as you want! You are the boss! When that money starts to roll in, I bet you won't want to stop.

This book is designed specifically for those of you who want to improve your present financial position. It will motivate you to take the first step along the way to certain success. As the late, great Vince Lombardi said, "The difference between a successful person and others is not the lack of strength, not a lack of knowledge, but rather a lack of will." This book shows you how to discover your own money-earning potential and to put it to work for your special benefit. You will learn numerous ways to turn your everyday activities into money-earning opportunities with little extra effort on your part. *Part-Time Income Enterprise* will describe hundreds of successful part-time, income-producing businesses.

You don't even need to step out of your own home if you don't want to. Nor do you need to sacrifice large amounts of time. This book will not only show you how to earn good money, but how you can have fun doing it.

Part-Time Income Enterprise is geared specifically to success in second-income ventures. It shows you how to turn every minute of your free time into money with proven examples of others who have put it to work.

You will become acquainted with a teenager named Brad, who was considering taking a part-time job to earn a little cash. When his mom's friends began admiring a birdhouse he had made her for a gift, he had a better idea. He thought of a way to make extra money on his own terms.

Brad received many compliments for his first birdhouse. So he decided to make several more for a local craft show. He quickly sold them, and a new business was born. Every birdhouse he sold was like a tiny, traveling advertisement. Everyone who saw one of his creations wanted to buy one.

Brad's birdhouses are made entirely from recycled and recyclable products. High-grade exterior paint makes the houses weather-resistant. The easy-to-remove bottom makes cleaning easy. Each birdhouse's design is unique. Most of Brad's ideas come from his imagination. He also takes special orders. Many customers even requested a birdhouse miniature of their own home.

Brad continued to operate his craft venture through high school and into college. His building took place in his spare time in the evening and on weekends. He really built a lot of birdhouses on school breaks and summer vacations.

Of course, running a business has it challenges. You have to motivate yourself to get the work done. Still, Brad would rather be his own boss than work for someone else. Brad has found personal satisfaction in his spare-time venture, along with earning enough money to buy a used car and a lot of spending money.

Like lots of kids, thirteen-year-old Jessie wanted to make some extra money.

She didn't want to sell homemade items or cut grass. She lived in a neighborhood where a lot of new homes were being built. Her idea was to clean those houses after the work crews left. So Jessie started "Neat & Pretty." Her business cleans houses during and after the construction process.

Jessie believed that builders would be interested in her services, but first she needed to let them know what she could provide. So she set up a marketing campaign. Most of her advertising was word-of-mouth, but she also sent letters and business cards to builders in her area. A few days after mailing out information, Jessie phoned the builders. She explained what she did and how she could help. She also cleaned a few houses for free to prove that she could do a good job. (Once they saw the great job, they offered to pay her.)

Before setting prices, Jessie contacted several local cleaning companies to find out what they charged. Jessie then set her prices slightly lower than her competition. She also gave special discounts.

"Neat & Pretty" offers three stages of cleaning:

1. The initial cleaning is done after the frame of the house has been built. It includes collecting bits of wood and shingles.
2. The drywall cleaning is done after the sheetrock has been installed. It includes picking up scrap insulation and electrical wire.

3. The final cleaning takes place after the building is completed. It includes picking up carpet pieces. It also includes vacuuming, mopping, and cleaning windows and fixtures.

A recent final cleaning took Jessie about three hours. She earned $150.00.

How about William? He started a cooking school as a sideline venture in one of the prosperous communities near his home. He picked a location convenient to all the wealthy people in that area and set up classes specializing in gourmet cooking. William held the classes two nights a week and charged a weekly fee of $35.00 for each student. With thirty or more regular students, he earned a considerable amount of extra income ($1,050.00 a week).

He specialized in gourmet dishes, wine, and cocktail selections and also focused on attractive methods of serving. Equipment and supplies needed for this venture vary, depending on how elaborate you want to be in the beginning. He needed at least a good set of pots and pans, plastic plates, spoons, and forks (for tasting) and food supplies.

William gave his students copies of the recipes he used in each lesson. He taught in a room leased in a business building. (If you don't mind, and you want to copy William's model, you could teach in your home, where you already have most of the equipment.) Since most of your students probably like to entertain and show off their homes, you could rotate to a different house each week.

These two teenagers and William are proven examples of how *Part-Time Income Enterprise* will help you turn your free time into money. Our program of result-producing step-by-step instructions, along with numerous examples of successful part-time ventures will take you from a low-capital beginning to a top money-making venture.

For many extra income ventures, there are skills you need that you may not even have thought about. It is important that you have a plan and some practice so that you are ready.

This book is intended for individuals who are planning to earn an extra income. This information is meant to be practical and relevant. You should feel that there is some real value in every activity you undertake. The exercises are designed to enable you to find out where your skills and interests lie.

The organization (format of this guide) was developed to allow for the presentation of one principle at a time with more advanced principles being reached only after basic understandings have been established. Topics have been arranged in the order that they will be needed. The numerous and varied activities will give you the opportunity to apply the principles studied, as you strive to reach your extra-income goals.

I would like to end on a personal note. This information has evolved from the influence of many people over many years. I am convinced that step-by-step development of subject matter, simple discussion, and generous practice will enable you to progress to where you "Can and Will" build your part-time venture faster than even you thought possible.

This is your personal success journey. As you go through this book, you will be asked to complete various exercises, which will assist you in analyzing your value system, establishing your priorities, reviewing your personal assets, skills, and talents, identifying your dreams, desires, and goals in life and developing your plans to achieve them.

Use this workbook. The forms are for your benefit and personal use. You do not need to share the results of your analysis with anyone else, unless you want to. Be totally honest with yourself, as you complete these exercises. This will give you maximum benefit in your search for extra-income success.

Use the opportunities presented throughout this book to help you define your concept of success.

This book will help you:

1. Determine the choices of life you are faced with.
2. Work out priorities in life in making these life-determining decisions.
3. Determine what success means to you.
4. Evaluate your personal skills, talents, abilities, resources and learn how to improve them.
5. Learn how to find your path to success and stay on it.
6. Determine what specific knowledge you have or require for your chosen extra-income venture.
7. Learn how to make your dreams a reality.
8. Learn what the roadblocks to success are and how to avoid or overcome them.
9. Learn the basic traits that successful people have and how you can develop them.
10. Learn how to multiply your time.
11. Learn how to get ahead in your extra-income venture.
12. Learn from stories of how others achieved success with their extra-income ventures beyond their wildest dreams.

Being successful, highly successful, in whatever extra-income venture you chose will not come easy. It will require hard work, concentrated effort, determination, and persistence. The old adage—"If at first you don't succeed, try, try again"—is so very true. Don't expect results overnight. Success in your extra-income venture will become a way of life. It consists of achieving one small success after another, of continually improving and raising your goals higher, each time you achieve a goal and, before you know it, you will be earning all the extra income you wish to earn.

The Quick List Exercise

This exercise will serve as a way of rapidly revealing your unconscious desires to yourself. There is something about being told or telling yourself to write down your thoughts or desires very quickly that seems to disarm the inner censor (the reticular activating system). The censor lets down its guard and, in seconds or minutes, you can discover things about yourself that you may never have suspected.

Now, quickly, write down three things you want most at this very moment. Don't stop to think. Just scribble your wishes down on the following lines.

1. _____

2. _____

3. _____

Now, read what you have written. Have you learned anything about your desires?

Variation: What would you like to do to earn your extra income?

1. _____

2. _____

What would you do with this extra income?

1. _____

Write, without stopping to think...

1. The happiest day of your life - _____

_____

Can what you did on the happiest day be something you could do to earn extra income?

Here's the link to my site, **www.parttimeincomeenterprise.com**, where you will be able to down load free the forms in this book.

Use the secured down load password — Free Forms

 Scan this barcode with your smart phone and it will take you to my web site www.parttimeincomeenterprise.com where you will be able to down load the forms.

Take some time now to fill out the WISH LIST

WISH LIST

MY DREAMS, DESIRES AND GOALS ARE:	PRIORITY RATING SCALE									
	1	2	3	4	5	6	7	8	9	10
1										

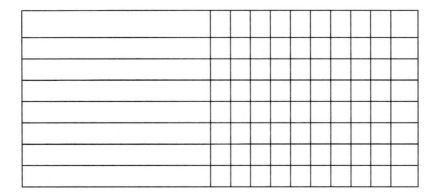

YOU MUST SET GOALS TO
REACH THAT EXTRA INCOME

Setting a goal can never be overlooked if you expect to be successful. A man without a goal is like a ship without a rudder. You can't head for a destination until you know where it is. Until you know where you are going, you won't know what road to take, or perhaps even more important, which one not to take.

- What do you really want? _____
- What do you need this extra income for? _____

What do you want to buy but can't afford? Below are examples write down what you want.

1. A new car _____
2. New furniture _____
3. A new house _____
4. A dream vacation _____

Add them all up. Contact the salesperson and figure out what the payments will be. Now you have a definite goal.

However you figure out what you want your extra income venture to accomplish, be sure to write the goal down by when you want it done.

GOALS THAT ARE NOT WRITTEN DOWN ARE JUST WISHES
WRITE YOUR GOAL DOWN _____

_____

Remember, you can't change the direction of the wind, but you can adjust the sails to always reach your destination.

Kreg was a teacher and had his summers off. His son was on a traveling baseball team. Kreg decided he needed to earn an extra $500.00 a month, starting in the middle of July, to help pay for his traveling expenses. He wrote down his monetary goal, along with the date on which he wanted to achieve it. Kreg painted homes on the weekends while he was in college. He decided the summers would be an excellent time to get back into the painting business. Kreg was getting older, now, and much wiser. He still enjoyed painting but found several other teachers with painting skills who were looking for extra income. He found house-painting jobs for them and took home an extra 20 percent fee for lining up their painting jobs. By having a goal and a plan, Kreg was able to enjoy the time with his family while watching his son play baseball.

HOW ARE YOU GOING TO ACCOMPLISH YOUR GOAL?

YOU MUST ASSESS YOUR PERSONAL ASSETS, ABILITIES, AND RESOURCES

What do you have to work with right now, today, as you start your path to earning extra income?

Before going any further, fill out the self-evaluation form on the next page by writing down all of your personal assets, abilities, and resources.

- Personal assets
- Skills, talents, and abilities
- Knowledge/know how
- Specific skills
- Specific talents
- Resources

Be totally honest and objective with yourself when you complete this form. When you finish, if you know someone that you feel comfortable with (a family member does not usually work well) and have a high respect for their opinion, ask him or her to review it. An objective second opinion may identify something you were not aware of. Accept the person's response graciously as constructive criticism. Remember, this extra-income venture is of utmost importance to you. You must stay positive and focused on your goals. No one is perfect. There is room for improvement in everyone. The successful person is one who, when he or she becomes aware of a fault, accepts the fact and does something about it.

Now fill out the self evaluation form

SELF EVALUATION FORM										
	SCALE FOR EVALUATION									
PERSONAL ASSETS	1	2	3	4	5	6	7	8	9	10
Untapped Potential										
Time (How Well Used)										
Freedom of Choice										
Intelligence										
Health										
Personal Energy										
Curiosity/Desire to Learn										
Persistence										
Dedication										
Determination										
Common Sense										
Positive Mental Attitude										
Discipline										
Imagination										
Guts										
Dreams, Desires & Goals										
Flexibility										
Beauty/Good Looks										
Judgment										
Self Confidence										
Reputation										

SKILLS, TALENTS & ABILITIES											
Communication											
Visualization											
Concentration											
Idea Generation											
Physical Strength											

KNOWLEDGE/ KNOW HOW	SCALE FOR EVALUATION									
(LIST BELOW)	1	2	3	4	5	6	7	8	9	10
SPECIFIC SKILLS (LIST)										

SPECIFIC TALENTS (LIST)											
RESOURCES											
Money											
Opportunities											
Material Goods and Property											
Income, Future											
Relatives											
Friends											
Credit											

You may be surprised when you find out you have more than you thought you had.

Here is my list of what you have, and I don't even know who you are.

1. **Untapped Potential:**

   Have you tapped your total potential? I doubt it. I have never met a person yet who isn't capable of achieving more than they think they can achieve.

2. **Time:**

   Did you write this down? It's one of your most important resources.

   Everyone has it, twenty-four hours per day. How you use this time can make the difference between mediocre and spectacular income.

3. **Ability to Communicate:**

   I know you have the basic tools of communication

   • You can speak.

   • You can write.

   • You can read.

   • But can you listen? This is the most important one.

4. **Freedom of Choice:**

   I assume you have the freedom of choice. The only constant in life is change. This is where you must look at your priorities in life and make that decision to earn that extra income.

   You now should have an idea of what you have to work with. This will serve as a basis for your search for an extra-income venture.

5. **What can I do?** You will want to take a good look at all your capabilities and decide what you do best and enjoy doing most. When evaluating your abilities, don't eliminate anything as too minor or insignificant. List everything you feel you can do with a fair amount of skill, and then decide which fits the following considerations best.

6. **Is there a demand for this?** This you can determine largely from observation.

   Many people are so caught up in their careers; they don't have enough time to do the regular things that need to be done around the house. They are willing to pay others to do it for them. Some examples are cutting grass, cooking, washing cars, and running errands along with taking the kids to ball games, etc.

Many people getting up in age can't do the above things, along with other simple things that are easy for most people, like washing windows, dusting, washing the dishes, driving to the grocery store or library, watering the flowers, and sending out birthday and holiday cards. Just use your imagination about the kinds of things you could do that other people can't do anymore, and you will be on your way to earning a large extra income. The best thing is, once you start these services, they will need and want you to do more and more.

(Remember to be good to your customers and give them what you have promised) **Happy Customers** *are your best advertisement, and their word-of-mouth is free advertisement.*

1. **Inquire among people you know and can become acquainted with through businesses or organizations about the marketability of your service or product.** Wherever possible, try it out on a small scale and see for yourself how it sells. As long as you are starting this as a second income, you can afford to try it out cautiously in the beginning. You should do this as thoroughly as possible before you invest a great deal of your time or money.

2. **What is the income potential from this?** You will need to figure as nearly as possible what your cost per sale will be for your product or service. Take the cost of the material you must use; then compute the time it will take you to complete it. Charge double that amount for your profit. When you decide how much time you can give to the operation, you will have a fair estimate of its future financial potential.

3. **How long will it take to reach this potential?** This should not be too difficult to estimate when you have worked out the details of step 2. Once you know how much time you can give to the operation and what your profit is for that time, it should be a matter of simple addition to determine when you can hope to reach your goals.

4. **How can I maintain myself while reaching that potential?** This will probably depend largely on how much work you can handle—after hours and for how long. You may want to take a look, also, at the possibility of turning this into a full-time operation somewhere along the line *before* it has reached its top potential.

All these considerations must be handled by each prospective business owner in his own way, but they should be carefully answered before the actual business operation is undertaken.

TIME
ORGANIZING YOUR FREE TIME FOR PROFIT

"This time, like all times,
Is a very good one,
if we but know what to do with it."
—Ralph Waldo Emerson

What to do with our time? This alone can make the difference between great success or mediocre achievement.

Everyone has the same amount of time—twenty-four hours a day. Have you ever noticed how some people can get so many things done, while others never seem to have enough time? You have enough time. It cannot be increased, nor will you lose any of it.

CHARACTERISTICS OF TIME

Time has some unusual characteristics that make it different from other resources.

1. Time exists only in the present instant.
2. Time is irreplaceable. (Once past, it is gone forever)
3. Time is effectively managed in the future. Plans must be made today for the effective use of time in the future.
4. Time tends to belong to everyone else.

Your time is demanded by your boss, your wife, your children, friends and neighbors, relatives, or even strangers. Without proper planning very little will be left for you.

Given these unique properties, it is very important that we use the time we have effectively and observe some rather well-established principles of time management.

These principles of time management are:

1. Know how you are spending your time.
2. Analyze your time and determine those activities that contribute to your goals and those that are not essential, or those that waste time and could be eliminated.
3. Plan your time for maximum effectiveness in getting those things done that have the highest priority.

Time management is the foundation for
achieving what you want out of life.
DON'T WASTE IT!!!

Know Thy Time

The first step is to gain an understanding of where your time goes

Before you can organize your time, you must take an inventory of your time. By using the TIME DIARY **(make a copy for each day of the week),** record how you spend your time for a week, including Saturday and Sunday. Record both time on the job, if you work, and your personal time. The form provides for a full twenty-four hours. It starts at 12:00 noon (you record sleep time too). Maintain this time diary throughout the day. Make it as accurate and detailed as possible. Be specific on what you did, so you can evaluate how well you spent your time. **This is very important, so stick with it.**

TIME DIARY		
Date _____ Day of Week _____		
TIME	**WHAT YOU DID**	**CATEGORY**
12:00 Noon		
12:15 PM		
12:30 PM		
12:45 PM		
1:00 PM		
1:15 PM		
1:30 PM		
1:45 PM		
2:00 PM		
2:15 PM		
2:30 PM		
2:45 PM		
3:00 PM		
3:15 PM		
3:30 PM		
3:45 PM		
4:00 PM		
4:15 PM		
4:30 PM		
4:45 PM		
5:00 PM		
5:15 PM		
5:30 PM		
5:45 PM		
6:00 PM		
6:15 PM		
6:30 PM		

6:45 PM		
7:00 PM		
7:15 PM		
7:30 PM		
7:45 PM		
8:00 PM		
8:15 PM		
8:30 PM		
8:45 PM		
9:00 PM		
9:15 PM		
9:30 PM		
9:45 PM		
10:00 PM		
10:15 PM		
10:30 PM		
10:45 PM		
11:00 PM		
11:15 PM		
11:30 PM		
11:45 PM		

TIME DIARY		
Date _____ Day of Week _____		
TIME	**WHAT YOU DID**	**CATEGORY**
12:00 Midnight		
12:15 AM		
12:30 AM		
12:45 AM		
1:00 AM		
1:15 AM		
1:30 AM		
1:45 AM		
2:00 AM		
2:15 AM		
2:30 AM		
2:45 AM		
3:00 AM		
3:15 AM		
3:30 AM		
3:45 AM		
4:00 AM		
4:15 AM		
4:30 AM		
4:45 AM		
5:00 AM		
5:15 AM		
5:30 AM		
5:45 AM		
6:00 AM		
6:15 AM		

6:30 AM		
6:45 AM		
7:00 AM		
7:15 AM		
7:30 AM		
7:45 AM		
8:00 AM		
8:15 AM		
8:30 AM		
8:45 AM		
9:00 AM		
9:15 AM		
9:30 AM		
9:45 AM		
10:00 AM		
10:15 AM		
10:30 AM		
10:45 AM		
11:00 AM		
11:15 AM		
11:30 AM		
11:45 AM		

Now You Must Analyze Your Time

After you have recorded a full week of time in your time diary, review and evaluate how well you spent your time. Categorize your time into the following groups:

- Productive time
  - Was it spent on achieving your goals?

- o Was it spent on achieving things *not* on your wish list, such as household chores, paying bills, etc., either on the job or off the job? How important were these activities?
- Rest and relaxation
  - o How much time was spent on sleep and other restful activities?
- Exercise and self improvement
- Idle conversation – not resulting in benefit
- Necessary functions
  - o This includes bathing, dressing and grooming, eating, etc.
- Travel time
  - o Time spent going to work, store, or other places.
- Entertainment
  - o This would include TV, going out, parties, dances, movies, hobbies, etc.
- Wasted time
  - o This would include unwanted interruptions by others, or time wasted by your own indecision.

The real benefit in recording time is to know what activities you spend it on. **By using the ANALYSIS OF TIME FORM, summarize your time for the week and total it up.**

ANALYSIS OF TIME								
CATEGORY	Mon.	Tues.	Wed.	Thurs.	Fri.	Sat.	Sun.	TOTAL
PRODUCTIVE TIME								
Goal Seeking								
Other On Job								
Other Off Job								
REST & RELAXATION								
Sleep								
Other								
EXERCISE								
SELF IMPROVEMENT								
IDLE CONVERSATION								
NECESSARY FUNCTIONS								
TRAVEL TIME								

ENTERTAINMENT								
WASTED / OTHER TIME								

Now, analyze it. How much time was spent on achieving your goals for your extra income venture? This is where you want to maximize your time. This is your priority use of time. Next, review each of the other categories.

Ask yourself, "How can I free up time for the things I really want to do?"

Do you need all that TV time, or has it gotten to be a habit? It is very easy to come home after an exhausting day and plunk down in front of the TV for the entire evening.

Wasted time can be a prime category for freeing up more time for the things you really want to do, like earn that extra income to buy a new car, a new carpet, a new house, or take a dream vacation.

Look at every category. Is it time you want spent this way? After thoroughly analyzing each activity, you are now ready to prepare a time budget.

You can go back and highlight items in the chart. How much of your week is under your control? Block out time for the job, related travel time, sleep time (how much you feel you need), and other nondiscretionary time. How much is left under your control? I bet you are surprised to find more than you thought. These are the groups of time you can plan your activities around.

You need to start organizing your time now, and you will discover the amount of free time you can find will be in direct proportion to how badly you want what you have set for your goal.

To organize your time, make a list of everything you need to do for the day. As each action is finished, mark it off the list. When you know what you must do in order of importance, the actual follow-through will be much simpler.

When you are organizing your time, it may be necessary for you to eliminate some frills and unnecessary activities from your routine. This should not be too hard, if your goal is important.

Plan your free time for the next few days. Write down and organize what you are going to do during your free time.

- "Turn off the TV," will probably be the first place to start for most people.
- Review interests, skills, and specific talents

Come up with some ideas of extra income opportunities that you feel might work for you. Write these down. This will be your wish or dream list. This should be a fun time. Let your imagination take over.

Stop procrastinating and start focusing on getting what you want. Your first priority should be getting things done as quickly as possible and as well as you can.

Margo discovered what she felt was a good extra-income venture. She decided to open a bead shop in a nearby shopping center on weekends. She enjoyed working with beads and making jewelry. She felt that there were enough ladies in the local area to keep her busy selling supplies two days a week.

To make sure, Margo began asking herself questions about whether this extra-income opportunity fit her own needs and desires. Margo discovered a few things. She discovered that she could probably turn a small profit while enjoying her venture, but that expenses would be high, and it might take her a year or two to build it up to a highly profitable venture. She had to cut expenses.

Her major expense, of course, was rent for a store that would be closed five days a week. She considered setting up the bead shop in her own home, but zoning did not allow that. Plus, she lived too far out of town to ask customers to travel to her. It would take too much expensive advertising to draw them out.

Studying the practicality of this bead store, Margo finally hit upon the answer. She would share a store with a related business. She soon found a major downtown market area that contained a large craft shop. She approached Edith, the owner, and offered to set up her weekend bead shop in the store and pay a percentage of her income as rent for the space. Edith saw the value of Margo's offer and accepted it.

During the week, Margo works as a training developer; but on the weekend, she is a successful bead shop operator, which she calls "A Passion for Fashion – Beaded Jewelry by Margo." She is a successful bead shop operator because she joined forces with another smart entrepreneur and built her extra-income venture.

THERE ARE THREE SECRETS TO ACQUIRING YOUR GOALS OF MAKING A SUCCESS FROM YOUR CHOSEN EXTRA INCOME VENTURE

1. Know where you want to go.
2. Know how to get there.
3. Then make the best of the situation when you arrive.

ARE YOU STRESS RESISTANT?

There are many stresses in your life now. Adding an extra-income venture could be another stressor.

How well do you manage stress? How committed are you to your work and life? Are you a risk taker? This quiz is a quick measure of your ability to resist stress through your use of these skills.

Score **0** if the statement is definitely not true for you, **1** if it is usually not true, **2** if it is somewhat true, and **3** if it is definitely true.

STRESS ASSESSMENT

1. ____ When I work hard, it makes a difference.
2. ____ Getting out of bed in the morning is easy for me.
3. ____ I have the freedom I want and need.
4. ____ At times, I've sacrificed for an exciting opportunity.
5. ____ Sticking to my routine is not important to me.
6. ____ I vote because I think it makes a difference.
7. ____ I make my own lucky breaks.
8. ____ I agree with the goals of my boss and my company.
9. ____ I've been "lucky in love" because I try to be a loving person.
10. ___ I believe I get what I *give*. But I don't keep score.
11. ___ It's important for me to try new things.
12. ___ Free time is a gift I really enjoy.

13. ___ I work hard, and I'm paid fairly.

14. ___ My family is a great pleasure to me.

15. ___ I speak up for what I believe in.

Scoring: Add your scores for #1, 6, 7, 9, & 13. This is your stress management score; the higher it is, the more control you feel you have over your own life, and the better you are able to manage your stresses. Total _____

Add your scores for #2, 3, 8,10, & 14. This is your commitment score. The higher it is, the more you are committed to and enjoy your life. Total_____

Add your scores for #4, 5, 11, 12, & 15. This is your risk score. The higher it is, the more willing you are to take risks. Total_____

ADD ALL THREE SCORES TOGETHER. THIS IS YOUR STRESS RESISTANCE SCORE.

Total_____

If you score thirty-five or above, you are very resistant to stress. Your attitudes help you. Congratulations! If you score from twenty-seven to thirty-four, you are somewhat resistant but could be more so. Look at each item, and choose a few to work on. If you score eighteen to twenty-six, you need to look at your habits and attitudes to improve your resistance to stress; go through the statements above, and pick one to improve each month. With a score of under eighteen, if stresses get serious, you could be in trouble; take time *now* to change your habits and attitudes; you may want to ask a professional counselor for ways to feel more positive about yourself.

Finding extra-income opportunities is not designed to add more stress to your life. It is our goal that you will find a satisfying and fulfilling venture that enables you to achieve your life goals.

We are now going to give you several business profiles; they are *not* going to be arranged by categories, because we want to keep your thought processes open. While reading one opportunity, you may be able to group its concept with another and come up with your own concept venture. Many extra-income opportunities will go into great detail, while others will only be examples of what others have done.

Please note that a business' profits are determined by many variables, and one's success will not guarantee your income success. This is why there will be no mention of get-rich-quick ventures. The ventures listed are realistic and proven ways to earn extra income.

IT IS NOW TIME TO SHOW YOU HOW OTHERS HAVE TURNED THE USE OF PART-TIME-INCOME ENTERPRISE INTO EXTRA DOLLARS IN THEIR POCKETS

Herb loved cars and trucks. He also had the skills to repair and detail them. Herb decided he would buy and sell used cars and trucks. He had to find profitable cars for sale, so Herb began scanning the newspapers, shopping centers, laundromats, for-sale-by-owner papers, and Craigslist for used-car bargains. Herb planned to sell the cars from his home (he would only buy and sell one car at a time), rather than using an expensive car lot. He would pull them into his garage and check out the mechanical and electrical systems. If they needed fixing, he would do that first. He then dressed them up by detailing them inside and out, ending with a waxing and buffing job. While Herb was out looking at the used cars, he also got a good idea of the price of different vehicles. He would always try to sell the car first by placing a For Sale sign in the window. Then he would run an ad on Craigslist and then in the newspaper. It didn't take long to turn a profit of $500.00 to a $1,000.00 since he knew his market. It all happened because Herb knew that planning was only part of success—doing was the most important part.

• • • • •

Ernie has a pick-up truck and attends large public market places, auctions, flea markets, and special sales. He has a sign he places on his truck with the word—HAULING, along with his cell phone number. He also has the ad on his T-shirt. Ernie just walks around and people call him. He loads his truck with their items and hauls it to their homes. Ernie develops relationships with auctioneers, antique dealers, etc. Many people have asked Ernie if he hauls trash. He never thought of that. Now he has added another service. He notes that it is important for people to be on the lookout for what is needed and make their services known to those who might want them.

• • • • •

Katrina and Jen worked in an office building and started to bring homemade sub sandwiches to work for their lunches. The sandwiches looked so appetizing, other workers wanted them. So the two young ladies got an idea. Why not take orders, make them, and bring them to work. It started with just a few orders, but in a short time, workers throughout the entire office building knew of the delicious sub sandwiches. When the orders came in, the ladies were making only $1.00 per sandwich profit but were making $60.00 extra a day. They learned the benefits of earning an extra income. They now are thinking of expanding to another building and having one of their stay-at-home friends make and deliver to that building. If this is the kind of extra-income venture you might be interested in, remember, you can add chips and drinks for extra profit. You need to check your city for food preparation laws.

• • • • •

As you can see so far, there is nothing special about any of these part-time-income builders. They saw a need and went for it. You can do the same and bring in extra income for your special needs. All you need to do is decide what you're going to do and how you're going to take that first step. Review your strengths and interests and start to build your extra-income plan now.

Need more ideas of how others have started earning income and what steps they took? Read on, and remember to keep your goal a new car, a larger home, more security, college education, or a better retirement in front of you at all times. Let's get started on finding out how others are making their dreams come true.

Ilene started a housecleaning service. She built this service very quickly from no clients to nine clients within weeks, just by word of mouth. To succeed in this type of venture, you must be very meticulous about details. I am not going to go into detail about how to start and run this business. You can read below and go to the website listed for more detailed information.

What we want to show you now is how her husband, Bonnie, spun off his part-time venture.

Ilene had predominantly females helping her in her part-time venture. By the way, it is now full time. Ilene's workers did not like to climb on ladders to clean windows, but Bonnie had no problem doing this. Guess what his part-time venture was? Window cleaning. You would not believe how many people hate to clean their own windows. Bonnie soon found out he could not keep up with the demand for cleaning windows. His trick was never to charge by the window (he did) but he never told the client that he charged anywhere from $15.00 to $30.00 per window. He counts the windows and multiplies it in his head and then tells them the price. This way it doesn't sound so expensive. Now, let's take it one step further. Bonnie has some friends help him clean the windows. He knows how long it takes to clean each window, so he tells his workers he is going to pay them a flat rate for the job. Whether it takes them one hour or three hours, they know what they are going to get paid. So if he has go-getters, we can see all the extra income he can make, since while they are cleaning, he can be out lining up more jobs. We are not going into all the details on how to clean windows. If you need more information, *Google* "Tips for Cleaning Windows," or Bonnie suggests *Googling* "Clean Windows with Vinegar."

You have decided you want to start a house-cleaning business and to clean homes professionally. Cleaning your own home and cleaning someone else's home professionally is totally different.

You have to be very thorough when cleaning professionally. Clients are paying you for a service, and they expect and deserve top-notch cleaning. It takes quite awhile to learn how to clean a home professionally.

The best thing to do when starting out is ask some friends and family members if you can clean their homes for free or at a discounted rate. I know the thought of cleaning for free is not appealing, but you will not only gain much needed experience; you will get some good testimonials and references (which you will need when you obtain those first clients).

When first starting out, don't worry about how long it takes to clean a home. Always do a thorough cleaning. After you have been cleaning for a while, you will become more efficient and will be able to do a thorough cleaning in a lot less time.

Make sure you have all the supplies and equipment needed before you start.

Supply List:

- window cleaner
- furniture polish
- anti-bacterial cleaner
- SOS pads

- stainless steel cleaner
- wood floor cleaner
- bathroom cleaner
- mops
- broom/dustpan
- supply caddy (home depot has some nice caddies)
- dust mop
- wood floor mop
- grout brush
- small toothbrush
- cleaning cloths (terry and micro fiber cloths)
- step ladder

If you would like to use all-natural aromatherapy products, try Signature cleaning products by Aromatherapy Naturals.

Start at the top of the home and work your way down. This cleaning routine is for a one-person cleaner just starting out. Of course, the routine changes with more cleaners. When you have more cleaners in the home, each person can be assigned different tasks.

- Empty all trash and replace trash bags
- Pick up/straighten/make beds if needed
- Remove cobwebs, dust baseboards
- Dust ceiling fans
- Clean window sills and wipe down doors
- Dust all furniture, including bottoms and sides
- Clean all glass surfaces, including smudges on windows
- Clean and disinfect bathrooms (dust light bulbs and wipe down cabinets)
- Sweep, vacuum, mop all floors
- Clean kitchen (including inside microwave, top of refrigerator)

- Wipe down kitchen cabinet facings
- Polish all glass surfaces and stainless steel in kitchen

For initial cleanings, include all the above, plus the following:

- Wet wash all baseboards and doors
- Clean all light fixtures
- Clean all wall hangings
- Clean all knick-knacks
- Clean vents
- Remove books from book shelves and clean

For move-in/move-out cleaning or real-estate cleaning, you will need to add cleaning inside refrigerator/freezer, oven cleaning and window cleaning, to your services. Also, for this type of cleaning, you should clean inside all cabinets and drawers and inside closets.

Here's the link to my site, **www.parttimeincomeenterprise.com**, where you will be able to down load more detail start-up information and plans

Use the secured down load password — Start-up plans

 Scan this barcode with your smart phone and it will take you to my web site www.parttimeincomeenterprise. com where you will be able to down load the free start-up plans.

Once again thank you for buying my book and good luck on earning the extra money you need to live the life style you and your family deserves.

How To Achieve Goals That Get Results!

In these uncertain challenging times, we must not give up on our dreams! Remember, goals are dreams with deadlines. The task of working on goals can be difficult, and we all need help. I've turned to Jim Ball for that help. Below is an article written by Jim to help you continue along the right path.

The Three Boxes in Life—By Jim Ball
Jim Ball, President, The Goals Institute

There are three boxes in life. Which one are you in?

Years ago, I took a screenwriting course taught by Rick Pamplin. Rick used a great metaphor he called the "Three Boxes in Life" to encourage people to pursue their passions. Box A is a big, beautiful box.

In Box A, you are doing exactly what you want to be doing. If you want to be an actor, you are acting. In Box A, you are, as the scholar Joseph Campbell put it, "following your bliss." Box B is a nice box, but it is not as big or bright as Box A. In Box B, you are doing some of what you want to be doing, while working toward being in Box A. If you want to be an actor, perhaps you are acting part-time, taking acting courses, and holding down another job to make ends meet. In Box B, you are not where you want to be yet, but you have a plan to get there and you are making progress.

Box C is a small, dark box. In Box C, you may be making a living, but you are not, as the motivator Les Brown puts it, living your making. If you want to be an actor, you are not acting or taking acting courses. You are spending each day doing something besides what your really want to be doing.

You do not have to have a goal of going to Hollywood to benefit from Rick's Three Boxes in Life metaphor.

If you find yourself in Box A, then great; there is nothing more to do. Just stay on course.

If you find yourself in Box B working a plan toward Box A, that is okay, too. Just make sure you are following a good plan with solid goals and an aggressive timetable to get into Box A.

If you find yourself in Box C, however, do not waste a moment. Immediately leap toward Box A. Using Rick's example, if deep down inside you want to be an actor and are not acting or learning about acting, then do whatever you must to get immediately on track toward becoming an actor.

I have related this metaphor to many people. Occasionally, someone will say it is too risky to leap abruptly from Box C to Box A. Yes, there is risk involved; however, life is brief. I think the greater risk is not in leaping from Box C to Box A; the greater risk is staying in Box C and not leaping. Copyright © The Goals Institute

If you're like most people, you are very excited and eager to move forward while you're reading this. Let's share how some others have earned their extra income.

Marvin was a very social person. He always enjoyed planning his family reunions. He decided he could earn extra income by bringing people together. As a reunion planner, he decided he could arrange get-togethers for high schools, colleges, or other institutions, as well as families and members of former military units.

Because many people no longer have the time to plan these events themselves, Marvin thought this was how he was going to make his fortune. He decided his service would organize all the events leading up to the reunion day, including locating classmates, family members, etc. (This has become a little easier with the help of online networks like Classmates.com and Plaxo.com), mailing the invitations, hiring the entertainment, finding the location, and taking reservations. A spin off business, which his wife ran was to provide items such as memory books, T-shirts, photo name tags, etc.

Starting out with his own family reunion, Marvin learned what was needed to make this extra-income venture work. A computer and Internet service was a must. He found out he could charge a per-person fee, based on the number that attended the reunion. To be like Marvin, you must pay attention to details, especially if it is going to be themed or if you want to relate it to what was current for that graduation year. Be sure to plan activities that will include everyone attending. Schedule appropriate entertainment, and make sure the space you are renting is large enough to handle the number of people that will be attending.

You must be able to market your service, design attractive, attention-getting mailings. You must contact high school and college class members, large families, former military units, and don't forget your church. Ask the suppliers (caterers, photographers, banquet hall owners, florists, etc.) to recommend your service. Don't overlook press releases and announcements in both print publications and online reunion Web sites. Start small. Provide great service and give more than is expected, and word-of-mouth will be your best advertisement. Search www.reunions.com for more information on this type of extra-income venture.

Let's look at a spa treatment that you can offer to people in their homes.

SPA in A Box, or The Pampered Lady. Here is the concept. You get the ingredients you need and combine them into a kit that you market to individuals who will take it to customers' homes, something like a home-decorating party. Your host would invite their friends over for a SPA evening. (Their cost will be determined by the cost of your kit and how much they would like to make) To see what works best, have some parties for your friends for free. They will have some fun, make plenty of suggestions, and realize they could be your first representatives. You could start with some nice, relaxing music and candlelight. The ladies would start by tensing and relaxing different body parts (you would lead this activity). This would be done as a group. You could then have some plastic tubs for a nice foot soak, using your special soak (this could be liquid dish soap with some aroma added, which will make the feet very soft). This is how you start to brand your own products. While their feet are soaking, you could serve some wine or a nice cleansing beverage. Some could have cucumber slices placed on their eyes or hot towels over their faces. You then take one set of feet out, dry them, and then apply some cream and provide a gentle rub. I hope you see where we are going with this. Depending on the number of clients you have, you may need to bring more representatives with you. Everyone loves to have his or her head rubbed; there are many wire manipulators on the market. These will not mess up the hair. If you wanted, you could soak their hands and paint their fingernails. You want this to be a fun night at home for the ladies at a reasonable price. Depending on how you want to go, you could have male representatives helping you out. This is a concept that we are leaving open-ended for you to run with. If you choose to take it and run with it, please contact the blog and let us know how you're doing. This might be a great way to get more representatives around the world using and selling your products. This way, you now have multiple streams of income.

- Hosting your own spa in parties
- Selling and promoting your own line of products through your representatives (you can sign up reps for free or charge them a small fee or percentage of what they bring in) This depends on whether you want to make money by selling your products or if you just want to sell your idea and marketing plan.

You must think **big** if you want **big** things to happen.

Margaret, a retired business teacher, who loved to travel, was finding that traveling cost more than her budget could handle. She enjoyed typing, and her speed was a respected eighty-five words a minute. She had a good command of English and could work well with people. Margaret decided she would work out of her home and offer a typing service as her part-time venture—The Electronic Office.

Margaret had to identify a need. She needed to find what her potential customers were looking for and how she could best fill that need.

She needed to identify who her potential customers were:

- College students' resumes, term papers, theses
- People who lost their jobs due to the economy and needed to update their resumes
- Business mailing lists, labels, and letters
- Contract proposals
- Manuscript retyping for writers

She was on her way. Margaret knew her venture would work when she estimated the market size that needed her services. The last time I talked to Margaret, she was starting a referral business for her typing service. You see, she knows many other retired business teachers and high school teachers that are looking for some extra, part-time income. Many college students are very busy and are willing to pay for typing services. If you go into this type of business, you will need to see if you want to make less of a profit from students, and realize it will probably be last-minute work. Or you need to decide if you should market your services to business or professionals. With all the work out there, all you need to do is choose the right opportunity for you. With her PC and the Internet, Margaret has even worked while she was relaxing on a Mediterranean cruise.

• • • • •

Elizabeth is a widow, CNA (certified nurse assistant) and church-going lady. She is a very social person that has held many part-time jobs, working in day care and cleaning homes. She felt the need to do more, something fulfilling. One Saturday morning, Elizabeth was in the grocery store watching an elderly lady struggle with her bags. The light went on in her head. Some call it "the Ah-Ha! Moment." She would work with the elderly and provide the following services:

- **Companionship**—A smiling face, a helping hand, ears to hear, and a voice to encourage. From conversation to cards, from reading aloud to going for walks, Elizabeth would focus on providing social and physical stimulation to keep people active and engaged.
- **General Assistance**—Everyday living activities such as housekeeping, laundry, preparing meals, sorting through the mail, or organizing personal affairs often present challenges to people. She would assist with household responsibilities, making life easier for her clients.
- **Personal Care**—Being a CNA, Elizabeth would be able to provide dressing, grooming, hygiene, and transferring her clients from a bed to a chair, or chair to a toilet, things that most people take for granted. These and other personal care activities can often be challenging to people as a result of age, illness, or injury. She realized that she could provide the assistance and encouragement these elderly people needed.

- **Transportation**—Whether getting to and from appointments, running errands, visiting the beauty parlor/barber shop, or enjoying lunch at a nearby restaurant, Elizabeth accompanies her clients, while they are away from home, and then she helps them get settled when they return home.

It seems like Elizabeth found herself a satisfying part-time-income opportunity. Indeed, she has! She is now running a full-time business that provides in-home care for the elderly. It has grown so fast, she employs twelve other CNAs. She is growing slowly, because she is a person who really cares about people and will not hire or place just anyone in a home. They must share her values. This is probably one reason she has enjoyed such success.

How could you expand this service?

New Moms and Working Parents
Provide an extra hand around the house for new parents after the baby's birth. You could also help working parents by staying home with sick or injured children in an emergency so parents won't miss work.

Recuperative Care
Allow clients recovering from illness or injury to resume their normal activities as quickly as possible.

Are you up to the challenge of doing what other people cannot do, doing the extraordinary? This is what is needed for you to become successful in making a go of your extra-income opportunity. I suspect Elizabeth's attitude is typical of every successful person named in this training program.

Part-Time Income Opportunity Mentality

Given Elizabeth's experience, and her recent business success, I asked her to give you some tips for success. Here is what she said:

1. **Eliminate self-limiting thoughts.** More often than not, people have preconceived notions about what is possible for them to achieve. They sell themselves short. Abolish thoughts that hold you back from achieving your true potential.

2. **Optimize your skills.** Everyone begins at a different place and each of us is dealt a different set of genetic cards. Use that to your advantage and optimize your assets.

3. **Be willing to spend the effort and energy to be successful.** Anyone can succeed if he or she is willing to work at it. Too many people want to reap rewards without the sacrifice that is necessary to achieve any goal.

4. **Enjoy the journey.** If you can enjoy the pursuit of excellence, you've got it made. Aiming to enjoy only the end result makes it impossible to endure the necessary sacrifices to achieve any goal really worth having.

    - **Be a student.** The more you understand about what it is you're trying to do and how to do it, the easier it is to be successful. Be a student of your passion.

    - **Persevere.** There are many things that can get in the way of successfully achieving any goal. You have to be willing to figure out how to get over, under, around, or through those obstacles. Keep trying.

    - **Develop mental toughness.** It is not the physical challenges that keep you from successfully creating your part-time venture; it is mentally giving up. You need to start believing that you can do it and that you can be successful. Others have been successful before you, and you can do it too.

- **Be prepared to suffer.** When you are striving to make a go of your part-time venture, realize it is a long haul. There is going to be set backs and times when you are just plain tired. Know that some stress, followed by rest, will make you stronger, physically and mentally.

- **Take strength from others.** This tip is particularly valuable for you when you start to think you took on too much. Right when you are thinking that things are really bad for you, look around. You'll see that others have made their part-time ventures work. Knowing you're not the only one who will experience setbacks and that other people worked through them generates energy, if you're willing to accept it.

You must want success. Doing something that is difficult requires that you want to be successful with every fiber of your core. The intense desire to succeed helps you overcome obstacles that crush other people. And that is all that Elizabeth had to say about that.

"Open Your Mind…Dare To Dream Again"

As we get older, instead of expanding, we tend to actually close down mentally and try to protect ourselves against disappointment. It's safer not to have too many dreams, because it's easier to avoid disappointments that way. Where you are right now might not feel that great, but it sure beats feeling disappointed! It sure beats having your dreams and hopes dashed against the rocks, or worse, feeling stupid or ridiculous for having hoped in the first place! The problem with mentally circling the wagons as you get older is that you close yourself down to the very thoughts that will change your life.

Since everything starts in your mind, then you must be willing to open your heart and mind to a flow of new ideas; otherwise, you'll just keep getting what you're already getting. And chances are, you wouldn't have read this far if you felt 100 percent satisfied with the condition of your life at this point in time. Sure, we all want to avoid disappointment.

We all want to keep from feeling hurt....or stupid...or ridiculous.... or wrong...or any of the negative emotions all of us have experienced (and will experience again and again, if we're living fully). But, unless you can form a new vision in your mind of what you want and why you want it, you'll never get anything meaningful out of life.

Unless you open yourself up to new ideas, new people, and new ways of thinking, you'll never get the new thoughts you need to make positive changes in your life.

It just won't happen. So dig those old dreams back out...even the ones you're too afraid to admit, even to yourself, let alone a friend or a spouse. Don't hide those dreams. Pull them out and take a good hard look at them.

Did you realize you can have anything you want if you simply think about it often enough and have a strong enough reason why you want it? It's true, because those two factors, desire and purpose, will drive you to take the necessary actions to achieve any goal!

So don't hide from your dreams or bury them in the back corners of your mind! Pull them out and keep them right there in front of you. Charge them with the power of your consistent thoughts and actions, which will, in turn, bring them into your everyday reality without fail!

In fact, **DREAM BIG**!

Dream as big as you can! Dream so big that, even if you only got halfway to your goal or desire, your life would be totally unrecognizable from where it is right now!

Ask and you shall receive; it's a Universal Law that cannot be broken, so do yourself a favor:

Ask for something really good!

Your life may not be where you want it to be right now…Your life may totally suck…Your life might be boring…You might be poor… You might have a heart condition…You might be a cancer survivor… You might have had severe asthma as a child…You might have adult ADD…You might hate where you live…You might drive a ten-year-old car…You might work for a boss who is an idiot…You might not have any confidence in your ability to change things. In fact, your situation could seem totally hopeless.

But you know what? **None of that matters**.

What matters is that you can *change anything* you don't like about your life and put yourself on the path to success, simply by changing what you constantly think about. Some problems take longer than others to work through, sure. But with consistent thought and action— with a purpose—you *must* achieve success in your life.

With that formula, there's no way you can't succeed!

So do yourself a favor and burn the following into your brain. Read it every day…**memorize it**… and make it a part of your everyday thought process. It will literally change your life forever!

Your level of success and achievement in any area of life is in direct proportion to your ability and willingness to direct your thoughts into effective planning and organized action toward a specific goal, combined with a strong reason why you're doing it in the first place! Jim Edwards

Packing Service

I have known people who made quite a bit of extra income by operating a packing service for people who are planning to move. This service adds a lot of value to the people thinking of moving, and you can usually charge less than a moving company charges and still make a substantial amount of money. The supplies are simple and easy to obtain with very little investment. A liability insurance policy is also quite cheap for this type of business. Business licenses vary by area. You can run the service just on the weekends or your days off. It can easily bring in several hundred extra dollars a month.

Gift Baskets

I like this one because it is really simple. Just buy a wicker basket at your local dollar or discount store, and fill it with age-appropriate items, such as lotions, soaps, potpourri, etc., for women. I would stick with baskets for women only. You can make up one basket, determine your cost, and take it to your local grocery store, convenience store, gift shop, flower shop, car wash, etc., and see if they are interested in buying it at a wholesale price you set. If they are, then you can make up more baskets to fill the demand. Decorate the basket with a card for an upcoming holiday, such as Mother's Day, Christmas, Halloween, Valentine's Day, Secretaries' Day, Grandparents' Day, birthdays, and other various holidays. There is very little investment, because you only prepare one basket and take it to several different outlets to determine demand. There are gift basket franchises out there that to do very well. You certainly don't need a franchise, just a flair for making a pretty gift basket that you put together for $5.00; sell to the merchant for $10.00 which the merchant sells for $20.00. The people that buy the basket will definitely see the value in this product that you have taken the time to assemble and effectively package.

Paid Surveys

This is a really great way to make some extra money each month. I am a big fan of taking paid, online surveys. You can register for free with survey sites and start making a few extra dollars a month by completing surveys for them. Here are 2 that work well www.mysurvey.com and www.npdonline.com/indexb.php. They can be addicting and take up a lot of your time be careful.

Pet Sitting

Since I am a dog lover, I also like this one. You can take care of pets for people going on vacation. I usually recommend that you take care of them at your own home. Just be sure to take care of them, as if they were your own, and everything should be okay. Only do one pet at a time. You do not want to be accused of running a kennel. Motels charge an extra $50 to $100 per night for pets, assuming you can even find a motel that will take pets. This can be a very valuable service for those who know they are leaving their pets with a responsible person. All you do is feed them, keep water for them, play with them, and take them outside (on a leash) when necessary. It can be a real vacation for the dog, cat, bird, lizard or whatever. You do very little extra and to ask $20-30 a night is not out of line. Knowing their pet is taken care of by someone loving and responsible is of immeasurable value to most pet owners.

Kyle, is a high school student who maintains lawns, he lined up grass-cutting jobs and set the price per job then recruited student friends to do the work, making a percentage from each yard. Last year, he made $24,000.00—not bad for a high school student working part-time and having others doing most of the work.

Learn a Foreign Language

Nearly all employers now a days are looking for employees who can speak, read, or write a foreign language. This is a skill that has long been overlooked. Most employers will gladly pay bi-lingual or multi-lingual employees some type of extra pay or bonus for their skills. In addition, there are many opportunities for multi-lingual individuals to make part-time, extra income using their knowledge of different languages (besides English). Courts, police departments, government service agencies, schools, and hospitals are always looking for full-time or part-time language specialists. This skill requires no special degree or certification. All you need to do is become fluent in another language.

Use The Internet

The internet is viewed by many as being the fastest and easiest way to make money today. There are many money making opportunities ripe for the picking. The best part of it all is that these opportunities are available to nearly everyone.

With that said, I can't stress enough the importance of setting realistic expectations. Don't get lost in all the hype and don't expect to quit your day job in a short period of time. Remember these are part-time income opportunities. Know what you want, set the game plan in motion and take action. One of the benefits of the internet or using computers to generate your part-time income is that it lets you work from anywhere and on your own timeline. That in its self is a money saver.

The absolute easiest way to make money online is with Affiliate Marketing. You don't have to create a product, set up a shopping cart and merchant account, do customer service, work with clients, etc. It is very much like a commission based sales job where you earn commission on sales you refer. The difference is that you're doing it on line, without ever having to meet people in person. You simply recommend products and or refer people to specific merchants through the content on your website, e-mails or blog.

Brandon has his site up and chose corn hole games as his niche market. His site generates him around $400.00 a month and he does not sell any of his own products. (He started to manufacture his own corn hole bags but it proved to be to time consuming for only himself so he researched companies that met his quality standards and became their affiliates) This worked for Brandon because he knew how to design his web site and how to maximize his SEO content. That is information that lets your site rank well with the major search engines. Brandon also provides corn hole game rules, examples on how to set up tournaments etc. His site provides free information to the people that come to his site. They learned to trust him and realized his recommendations were valuable and the affiliate sites offered quality products.

Jim and Josh were always interested in computers and decided to start a computer repair business. Through word of mouth news of their repair business spread to friends and family and their acquaintances all wanted help with their computers.

- Fixing them
- Speeding them up
- Installing new programs
- Removing viruses
- General tune ups, etc.

Jim and Josh each approached their computer business differently. Josh was happy with word of mouth where he would get one or two jobs a month. He charged a little more than the cost of the parts. He eventually bought some business cards through www.vistaprint.com. This made him look creditable. His part-time business stayed part-time in his local community.

Now let's look at what Jim did. He started the same way Josh did by word of mouth, business cards, and flyers. Then he started to place small ads in the local newspaper and placing ads on community boards. This increased his business dramatically. Jim was very happy. He realized if he was going to increase his computer repair business he would have to be certified – Cisco certified or Microsoft MVP etc. Once he had some certifications, he made himself more professional looking and trustworthy. People don't just want to give their computers to anyone. There is a lot of personal information on them. Jim made a professional website, started a word press blog and started to make YouTube "how to" videos on care and maintenance of personal computers. This definitely positioned him as an expert authority on computer repair. He made himself available to speak at any club or event in the community. He became a member of the local Chamber of Commerce. Now not only is Jim fixing home computers, he placed himself as the "go to" person for many small businesses and individuals that have personal offices. He has now started to repair I Phones and has made quite a name for himself nationwide in this area. One of the main reasons Jim made himself and his business so successful was his ability to place himself as an expert by being on You Tube and using his blog. He also learned he doesn't know everything so he tries to keep his skills current. He visits web sites like CNET and ZDNET to update himself on new software applications. These sites also list technology webinars that are being offered. A sign of a good repair person knows where to go if you don't know something. Jim subscribes to the Experts Exchange and Microsoft's Experts Exchange where he pays a small yearly fee.

Now he has access to the tech community and usually receives a response to his questions in a few hours.

One thing Jim believes in is "don't work for nothing". Your time is valuable. Know what the going rate for computer repair is in your area and remember you are now an expert. Don't be afraid to demand a reasonable fee.

Create an E-book

If you have some special and extensive knowledge about a particular hobby, activity, or skill, then put it to use and write about it. Maybe you know several different ways to tie knots. Maybe you are really good at making homemade Christmas decorations. Maybe you have extensive knowledge about taking care of a sick loved one. Or maybe you know some special tricks in preparing meals for large or small families. Everyone has some specific and valuable knowledge about something. I can just hear you say, "I don't really know much about anything." My answer to you is "baloney!" You know a lot about several things, but you just don't realize it. Sit down and start talking with someone else about what you know. Pretty soon, you will realize that you really are an "expert" about something. Whatever it is, write a detailed and extensive "how to" manual about it. You can do it on the computer right there in front of you. Once it is written, there are several e-book publishers that will be interested in it. You can do a web search for "e-book publishers" or "e-publishers" and find many sources that will publish your information. Just don't get carried away and spend a lot of money getting it published. You are looking for a non-subsidy (you don't pay) royalty-paying (they pay you for sales) e-publisher. You can sell an e-book over and over again. If you only make fifty cents per sale, ten thousand downloads of your book will make you $5,000. The startup cost is just your time in doing the writing and possibly a small fee to get it listed with a reputable e-book publisher, or you can set up your own sales site. Remember, everybody knows something that can bring value to another person's life. Just think of the number of times you wished you had a detailed and clear instruction manual about some task you had to perform. If you have some idea that helps people, adds value to their lives, and you are knowledgeable about the subject and want to write an e-book and market it, then now is the time to do it.

Phil is making extra income working for banks that are foreclosing on houses. When people are put out of their house, many just pick up and leave. This leaves the bank with a clean-up job and no one on their staff to do it. Phil contacts the lenders and, for a flat fee, cleans up the trash left behind inside and out. Along with the fee, Phil can keep anything he picks up; this is how he creates another income stream—selling on Craigslist, yard sales, taking metal items to the scrap yard, or even placing items in consignment shops. He donates some items to charity or families in need from his church. The rest of the items are hauled to the landfill. As you can see, one man's junk can be another's treasures.

Then there is Tim, an avid hunter and fisherman from a small town. Tim loved to hunt pheasants on the farms near his home. The light came on for Tim one day and he decided to place an ad in a national sportsman magazine for pheasant hunts. He arranged for their state licenses, lodging, and he acted as their guide. Tim soon learned that many hunters from around the United States were eager to hunt pheasants. If you are short on funds, you could design a flyer and send it out to hunt clubs in neighboring states. You could make a video of a hunt and post it on YouTube. This will add credibility to your guide service. An added stream of income would make a pheasant cookbook, which you could sell or give out for free.

Are you an organized person? If so, you could promote yourself as a Professional Organizer. The opportunities let you service both residential and corporate clients. You would be helping them set up library and filing systems, in addition to general time and space management. Eighty percent of clutter is not due to insufficient space, but disorganization. People need to regain control of their surroundings, once again, which gives them peace of mind in their otherwise hectic schedules.

As a professional organizer, you will assist clients in their homes and offices helping them manage their time, papers, e-mails, space, clutter, and other aspects of their personal and work lives that need order. This can range from organizing kitchens, closets, home libraries, home offices, garages, computer files, and anything else that has gotten out of hand, as far as clutter and disorganization is concerned. Your target market could be the elderly, professionals with businesses in their homes, such as writers, researchers, business executives that maintain home offices, and people who work full-time and are involved with their children's activities and community projects. Many items once thought permanently lost often turn up when a professional organizer is at work, such as money, airline tickets, photos, jewelry, and other buried items. An extra income stream would be to write an e-book or produce a video on organizational tips that you could offer for sale. You want to be able to teach your clients how to stay organized through effective and easy-to-follow methods.

Craft promoter Kelly loves to go to home parties that deal with handbags, jewelry, beauty items, home decorating, etc. Her idea was to become the promoter. She contacted different vendors and scheduled for a fee a location where they could all set up their wares and demonstrate their items. Each vendor would have a half hour as a featured presenter. An example would be to charge each vendor $25.00 times ten vendors equals $250.00. Rent a recreation club house for $50.00, run an ad in the local paper for $35.00, and the total profit $165.00. Your real money will come from your snack bar, and if you work it with the vendors, you will be able to negotiate a free item or at least a percentage off of their items. Remember, you will be able to visit all of the tables and attend all the half-hour presentations and socialize with everyone.

Tutoring Service Kimberly is a teacher who realized that, with all the cutbacks in funding for education, crowded classrooms, and rising numbers of students dropping out of school every year, tutoring and remedial education services were needed in almost every school system in her area and probably the country.

- Elementary students: reading, writing, etc.
- High school students having problems with algebra
- College-bound students
- Students in college, adults wanting to brush up on their basic skills or preparing to go to college or return to college
- People in physical or drug rehabilitation programs
- New citizens wanting to get a better grasp of the English language
- Companies needing help for Hispanic employees learning English and grammar skills
- Students needing SAT preparation help
- Students applying for scholarships or filling out FAFSA forms for federal student aid

Kim decided to start her tutoring service out of her house, or she would travel to the student's house. It is very important to work closely with a student's teacher and have a checklist for the teacher to fill out and then give periodic reports to keep the communication open between teacher, student, parents, and tutor.

Remember, you can't be the expert in every subject. Your two hands can only generate so much income (or work with so many students at a time). You guessed it. You become the lead teacher, you recruit your teacher friends as tutors, and then you line them up with students, according to their specialties and interests. Once again, you will take a percentage of what they charge per student. Word-of-mouth is your best advertising, but you should register your services with all the schools in your area. Make sure you go to local churches and make presentations to civic groups. When approaching a church, you could lower your fee, if they will let you use their building for free. This would be a win-win for everyone.

As an added service, you could help with resume writing, cover letters, report editing, and proofreading services. You could offer job counseling, career exploration, and interview coaching.

As you can see, many of these extra-income opportunities lend themselves to **multiple streams of income.**

Multiple Streams of Income

Thirty-five years ago, you could probably get by with one income, the breadwinner, usually the man. Today, very few families can survive on less than two streams of income, which includes both husband and wife. In today's stormy economy, two streams aren't even enough. You'd be wise to have multiple streams of income flowing into your life. Why? If you only have one stream and you lose it, you are wiped out, and it will take you years to recover. Get the picture?

There are two types of streams of income: **Linear** and **Residual**.

If you get paid once for every hour you work, then this income is *linear.* Income from hourly or salary is linear. You get paid once for your effort.

With *residual* income, you work hard once, and it unleashes a steady income for months or even years. Yes, you get paid over and over again for the same work. A very simple example of this would be you have a bulk candy/ gumball machine you place it in a store and fill it up. Two months later you come and take out the money and refill the machine; that machine works for you for sixty days.

Another example is Vincent, who is a chiropractor. He spent one thousand hours writing his book on eliminating body pain before he made a single penny. High school students working in fast-food restaurants were making more money than he made. But Vincent wasn't looking for a salary; he was looking for a royalty. So he was willing to sacrifice his time, because he knew that, every time he sold a copy of his book, he would earn a royalty. His checks are still being deposited in his account ten years after that first check. Just like the candy machine, he doesn't have to be there! And the money flows without him.

Remember how these people earned extra income:

- Kreg the house painter recruited his friends to help him paint (he set up their jobs for a percentage of the job).
- Kim, the tutor, recruited her teacher friends to help tutor for a percentage. So, for every thirty-dollar tutoring job, Kim would make one or two dollars, which added up over the course of the year.
- Spa in A Box, where you would recruit representatives to market your brand, enables you to make a percentage from each sale

This is the power of residual income. By starting your extra-income opportunity, you are on your way to multiple streams of income. Let's say you are married and both you and your wife work. This is two streams of income. Your part-time-income opportunity is going to be painting houses; this is your third stream. Now, you are going to have your friends helping you; you are now on your fourth stream. Your wife purchases five vending machines and places them in five stores; this will be your fifth stream of income. Now, you can write an e-article on how you are making money with your part-time-income opportunities, which you then post on the Internet and make a royalty every time it is downloaded; this is your sixth stream of income.

Invest the money you earn from your extra streams of income into a dividend-paying stock, and have those dividends reinvested, earning you money without ever doing another thing with it. There you have it seven streams of income.

What you are looking for are multiple streams of income. This course is not designed to show you how to develop multiple streams of income. But it would not be fair to you, for us to help you start that extra income venture and not at least touch on how you could earn more and, more importantly, **keep more** of the money you will earn.

If you have read this far, you should have a good start on what your extra-income opportunity might be; if not, you may be a procrastinator; don't be overwhelmed in what you must do to start. It is normal to dawdle sometimes and stare out the window or go for a walk. That may be exactly what we need to do. All procrastination is delay; people procrastinate when they're not confident that they can complete a project, when they find it boring or distasteful, and when they're impulsive. You must make finding or starting your extra-income opportunity a *must*. When it becomes a *must,* you will take action; it must be *now*. How often have we said we'll check e-mail? It'll only take a minute, and three hours later, we're still on it. Technology provides us with immediate rewards without moving from our seats. We know that half the time people are online, they are procrastinating.

What are the secrets of overcoming procrastination? We know the more concrete a task is, the easier it is to get started. Breaking larger projects into immediate tasks is also helpful. Another step is putting temptations and distractions out of sight—for example, turning off the alert beep for new e-mails and structuring time to fend off distractions. For example, you can establish a ritual for doing e-mail in concentrated bursts at particular points in the day, not in inefficient dribs and drabs.

These tricks won't work for people who have a decisional type of procrastination.

It is now that you must decide when, and you must take a look at the goals in your life and say, **"This is what I want to do *now* to earn my extra income."** You must take responsibility. *If you cannot find a way, then make a way!*

Deciding on what income opportunity you want to pursue is not easy. There will always be obstacles, no matter what we try to achieve! Great rewards usually have great obstacles. We must have steadfast determination to make it happen. We must decide, now, what we want in life, why we want it, and what extra-income producing opportunity we're going start to reach this goal.

George Bernard Shaw, the writer, said, "People are always blaming their circumstances for who they are. I don't believe in circumstances. The people, who get on in this world, are the people who get up and look for the circumstances they want. If they can't find the circumstances they want, then they create them!"

You must take responsibility for your own successes and failures. You are totally responsible for what you make of your life. Remember, you are the master of your fate. You are the captain of your soul.

Ultimately, it is up to you to make your dreams into realities! Review your vision. Make wise decisions. Keep going after your dreams.

Example: I want my *(list you part-time income venture)* **(house painting)** extra-income opportunity to earn an extra $500.00 a month, so I will be able to provide my son the ability to go to football camp this July.

You have stated what you wanted; you know what the results will be. You now must start moving in that direction. Be passionate about what you do. It creates excitement, energy, and motivation. *As Zig Ziegler said, "You were born to win, but to be a winner you must plan to win, prepare to win, and expect to win."*

Let's look at how some others have created their part-time-income opportunities:

Trey, a full time educator part-time entertainer, is a magician who has a standard Saturday night show at one of the local restaurants where he does close up magic tricks at the tables. He also is available for parties and corporate events. Other options in this area would be clowns, face painters, balloon artists making animals etc. Your venues could be children and adult parties along with corporate functions.

Jan grew up on a dairy farm. She found her niche with her love of animals. She now has a traveling zoo. Jan has quite a collection of interesting and unusual animals. Jan visits schools, day care centers, retirement homes, birthday parties, and even corporate family events. The zoo is always a big attraction at the annual county fair. Jan also has special days when she has an open farm day where people purchase tickets to visit her home based zoo. Her daughters sell drinks, hotdogs, hamburgers and snow cones.

Chuck did the same thing but he specialized in snakes. At one time he had over 100 snakes. (As you probably guessed he was named the Snake Man) His traveling show was meant to educate and entertain at schools and parties.

Can you think of other specialties for your part-time income opportunity: pigs, turtles, ducks, chickens, rabbits and even pony rides?

Linda and Margo love to shop and travel. They organize van and bus trips. They plan the trip, advertise and act as guides on the trip. They organized outlet shopping, casino and theater shows. They are planning to offer theme park, sporting events and sightseeing tours in the near future. They have a lot of success with churches, schools and fraternal organizations. Sometime they have extra seats so they run an ad in the local paper and it does not take long to fill the bus.

They have a friend Robert who is a self proclaimed Southwest (USA) tour guide. Linda and Margo set up the trip with Robert who plans the itenery. The travelers fly, drive or ride a train say to Phoenix AZ where Robert, Linda and Margo meet them and the tour begins.

Linda and Margo figure in the cost of their trip along with their profit when pricing the trip. This means they travel free. Once the trip, legwork and contacts are made, it just comes to marketing.

If you like professional baseball your specialty could be baseball. Travel specials to professional games, spring training games, and triple A ball games (these games are very exciting and extremely fan friendly). There are many people who want to visit all the major league baseball parks on their bucket lists. Your part-time business could make these dreams come true for them. While making your own dreams come true. Speaking of bucket lists, you could be the CEO of the Bucket List. Many people have a bucket list and that is all it is-- just a list, but never acting on the list. You could make theses dreams become a reality.

Craig's sister, Janice wanted to have a major food fight on her bucket list. Craig was going to make this happen for her on her 38th birthday. He went out and purchased 10 gallons of ice-cream, 24 cans of spray whipped cream, 16 apple and cherry pies, 6 cans of spray cheese, 6 watermelons, 20 pounds of mashed potatoes, 5 gallons of blueberries, and 8 pounds of multi colored sprinkles. Craig also told everyone he invited to also bring at least one food item they would like to throw. The date was set. He brought 3 video cameras and set them up outside in his back yard. After the birthday cake was cut the food fight began. Yes, the cake was the first food item to be thrown. As you could imagine it was a sight to behold. His sister was very happy and everyone involved had a great time.

Yes, there was a large mess but several garden hoses took care of it. Everyone involved had their street clothes on and it was a sight to behold and best of all it was captured on video and copies after editing were mailed to all involved. Hint; try not to schedule the food fight on a real hot day. Bees could be a problem. You may be thinking all that food was expensive and a waste of good food. The smile on Janice's face made it all worth it. Now your job as Bucket List CEO is to see how you can help people get thru their bucket list.

Jeremy loves Thanksgiving; he also likes to deep-fry turkeys. He has three deep fryers and one large tank of propane gas. He sets up outside his garage, and the people on his street bring him their turkeys, and he cooks them for them. He charges them by the pound. (he figures in his time and the cost of the gas and cooking oil). If you do what Jeremy does you will learn how to cook the turkeys, and not have a mess. This is a large inconvenience that most people don't want to deal with. You must dispose of the used oil when you are finished cooking. Once you have the oil hot, it won't take as long to cook the other turkeys. Take orders and assign drop-off and pick-up times.

Jeremy and his friends also like to tailgate at his university football games, so he decided to go early and set up his cookers before the game. You guessed it; he started to take orders to cook the other tailgaters' turkeys.

He branched out and started to deep fry whole chickens, which proved to be a large draw and took a lot less time. Jeremy outfitted a trailer for easy transportation. He plans to add more fryers as his business expands.

He is also considering branching out for parties and picnics. If interest grows, he is looking at starting a turkey-frying business opportunity, where he will build trailers (or sell the plans on how to build them) and add the number of fryers requested, and then offer a business operating manual and marketing plan for a flat fee.

Caron is all about relaxation. She calls her part-time venture "The Relaxation Station." She has outfitted a used RV with vibrating, relaxing/massaging chairs. She has a set time to park outside office buildings and passes out flyers to the employees that schedule fifteen-minute relaxation power naps. (Caron has relaxing music playing in a semi-darkened area). She also serves bottled water and juices and charges a flat rate. She is going to try to make proposals to the company owners, showing how this rest period will increase employee productivity. She is also looking to offer chair massages in the future.

How about setting up a mobile dog-washing business!

How about a door-to–door dry cleaning delivery service (subcontracting for a dry cleaner for a percentage)?

Create a plant-watering or garden-watering business.

Sell an old family recipe, your grandmother's spaghetti sauce at $3.00 each.

Mark is an avid photographer, who also loves animals. He decided to operate a Pet Photography, part-time-income venture. Research shows that many photographic studios will consider photographing a pet. However, they do not openly welcome your furry family members. Mark decided he would specialize and welcome pets; in fact, he states that pets are his only business. His advertisements state, "We are dedicated to capturing a moment with your pet you can remember forever, to preserve that special relationship." Mark is operating as a home-operated, part-time sole proprietorship. He has hopes to be able to expand into a full-time business. He offers portrait sittings in either his well-equipped studio, the comfort of the client's home, or in an outdoor setting. Research showed many of today's white-collar professionals, between the ages of twenty-six and sixty have at least one pet in the household. The pet is treated as a family member, and the owners spend approximately $26 billion annually for gourmet food, cosmetic services, health care, and specialty items.

Mark will be targeting clients in these markets. He also partnered with the pet-related services they use, such as grooming salons, specialty pet stores, and veterinary clinics. He placed brochures and framed pet portraits in these locations. He also works and supports the local humane society and helps local dog and cat specialty shows by providing free portraits for awards.

Mark expects a rapid increase in sittings during the holiday seasons and may even set up in the center of the mall during these times.

He states that the key to a successful pet photography venture includes a commitment to quality and customer satisfaction. You must be responsible for ensuring a high degree of professionalism in three areas:

- Consistent fulfillment of the client's expectations.
- Competitive pricing for the quality and array of services offered.
- A fair and reasonable profit on each portrait.

Sheila is an art student who specializes in fashion design; she is very good at this, but she soon found that just having a lot of nice pictures didn't do much for her. She and a few friends started to talk to Sheila's mother who was a seamstress, but the girls never thought to ask her to make some of her designs. Once she started to make some of them, the local high school students fell in love with them and started to buy them for the homecoming dances, ring dances, and then the prom. Word spread, and she was soon designing wedding gowns and the bridesmaids' dresses. Sheila did some research and found that many young professionals were interested in sewing but never learned the basics on how to sew. Sheila decided to open up a shop, where clients could come in and take sewing classes to learn how to sew. Soon, she was helping them with specific designs they would come up with. They welcomed the chance to use professional-quality sewing machines; she also offered the use of an embroidery machine.

Some clients just wanted to have a one of a kind outfit, and others welcomed the opportunity to display and sell their creations in Sheila's boutique. Sheila even sets aside one evening, when the ladies get together; she calls it "sewing buddies," and all the notions they buy are half price. People are getting more creative and want to express themselves, and classes are filling up quicker than ever. Sometimes, the clients would like to have private one-on-one lessons, and Sheila schedules them also.

Some additional ideas you could spin off with your sewing services could be:

Sewing:

- Baby clothes
- Baby-doll clothes
- Stuffed animals (bears)
- Custom cushions and pillows
- Curtains
- Alterations
- Costumes

Here are some examples:

Clint is a runner, and his wife Elona was tired of seeing his trophy shirts all over the house; his drawers were overflowing with T-shirts. Clint wanted a quilt with his favorite race shirts, but most commercial companies were very expensive. Since Elona and her mother could sew, they decided they would make the quilt for him for his birthday. When they found out how much fun it was working on it and how much he enjoyed receiving it, they decided on a part-time-income venture (making quilts). They knew most runners don't like to spend a lot of money, so they undercut the local quilt maker and, as they figured, the business started to pour in. Elona, stated, "if you are going to undercut someone's price, you must be sure that you provide better quality and better service." In this case it worked.

She took out adds in the local running clubs newsletters, made a website, set up a display at the local races, and placed flyers in race packets.

Another young man, Calvin, was a Civil War re-enactor and discovered a need for the uniforms and clothes that the women and children wore. He created a fulltime business just from this one area. His work was seen on the big screen when movies were made about the Civil War. He just happened to be in the right place at the right time and turned his hobby and skill in sewing into a very lucrative living, which lets him travel the country.

Remember you're in charge! It's true that there are some things we can't control. But there is so much we can! From your attitude and actions to your decisions and your dreams, you have the power to shape your today and tomorrow. Your life is in your hands. Make it great! Whatever you choose for your part-time income venture make sure you enjoy it and the money will follow.

What type of special talent do you have, where you could open up a studio or just offer classes in your garage?

Sam and his wife Molly were always watching *Home and Garden* TV; they decided they could offer classes on how to refinish and paint furniture.

Sam was good at refinishing, and Molly had a flair for design and color coordination. How would they get people that were interested to come to their garage?

- First they decided to place flyers on the bulletin boards at arts and craft stores like Ben Franklin's, Michael's, and Garden Ridge; they also made a deal with the managers of these stores that, if they would help spread the word, they would encourage the clients to purchase their supplies at their stores. The managers went one better and said they would offer a 10 percent discount. This proved to be a win-win for all involved.
- As more people started to come to the basic classes, there became a need for advanced classes. So they found Donna,

who would teach a one-stroke painting class, and Jan would teach stenciling. The students were excited and enjoyed the classes so much, they were running out of their own projects, so they would either work on their friends' projects (for a fee, of course); some would go to thrift stores and pick up furniture and then refinish it, and then they would get together and have a craft sale.

- Some of the ladies became so good at designing and painting, they hired themselves out and did freelance custom work in clients' homes and businesses.

This worked out for Sam and Molly, because they filled a need—people needed a creative outlet and a place to work.

Now, let's look at Judy, who is a fun-loving, outgoing lady who was looking for a little extra spending money. Judy thought she would deliver balloon bouquets for people's birthdays, promotions, and anniversaries. She said she could get started with a small investment, a basic box of balloons and a helium tank and some string. She would write and print the cards on her home computer. Judy made up flyers and posted them in businesses. It didn't take long for the phone to start ringing; customers thought it was such a novel idea. Judy was having so much fun doing this; she started to dress up as a clown and then started to make catchy poems or even singing a verse when she made her deliveries. Her business spread by word-of-mouth so fast, it was hard for her to keep up with the deliveries. It was a good thing she had a friend who would make up the arrangements, and Judy would make the deliveries.

Rita, like Judy, wanted to earn an extra income. Rita liked to eat ice cream, so her part-time-income venture would be to provide make-your-own-sundae parties. First, she thought she would do it just for birthdays, but she soon figured out the sundae parties would be an added treat for any type of party, including golf outings, swim parties, office parties, TGIF parties, girls' night in parties—any time a group of people wanted to get together. One lady invited her group of five families that regularly got together on Saturday night to a BYOB party (bring your own banana); no one had any idea what to expect. You guessed it; they made their own banana splits and had a great time. Once the word spread, Rita was an addition to many corporate functions. Rita found a need and filled it.

Dannie loved animals, and she had friends who had pets whose dogs were very large, and their parents often complained about how hard it was to load them into the family car and take them to the vet's. Dannie thought she could transport them. She started "The Pet Taxi," where she would transport dogs, cats, birds, etc. The most common destinations were to the veterinarian or for grooming appointments. She soon found out that many people wanted someone to drop off their pets at boarding facilities, when they went on trips. They also wanted her to pick them up and deliver them to the house when they arrived back home.

If you're interested in doing what Dannie did, you would be wise to have a van with air conditioning and cages or a rack where the crates could be securely locked in for safety. Dannie said she charges by the size of the animal and the distance traveled.

Dannie advertised by posting flyers and business cards on community bulletin boards. A sure fire method of advertising was to establish a working arrangement with veterinarians, pet groomers, and pet stores in her area. This way she could offer this service for her customers. These places could add this fee onto their bills then pay Dannie or just put her name and contact info on their printed material. Also, running small ads in the newspaper and word-of-mouth is the best form of advertising.

If you want to create more need, donate your services to the local animal shelter/SPCA, and try to get this listed in the newspaper in the local section as a community interest.

Dannie said her market was made up of busy people with full-time jobs, older people who couldn't transport their pets, pet owners who just didn't want to put their pets in their cars, since they might be too large. She also indicated that she picks up and delivers large bags of dog food and sometimes prescriptions. Her advice is you must be reliable and work sometimes without a schedule.

IF YOU HAVEN'T FOUND WHAT YOUR PART-TIME-INCOME OPPORTUNITY VENTURE WIL BE, YOU MAY WANT TO:

Raise your awareness as you go about your daily activities.

- What feels good when you're doing it?
- What leaves you exhausted?
- What sharpens your senses?
- What makes you smile?

Pay attention to your feelings when you're feeling them. Listen, also, to the compliments you receive. What may be obvious to your friends may be obscured from your vision of yourself. You find yourself not paying attention. Passion wakes us up. But first, you have to take notice. Discovering your passion is, of course, an ongoing process. Don't start a part-time venture just to start one to make a few extra dollars. If you're willing to make the effort to find those things that turn you on, some outrageous ideas may appear. Don't dismiss or ignore them. Realize that, as you become passionate about what your extra-income opportunity will be, the wildest dreams are the easiest to accomplish.

As soon as you trust yourself, you will know what your extra-income venture will be and when to start moving in that direction. Remember why you want to start this part-time, income-producing venture. What's your motivation? That dream vacation, new carpet or hardwood floor, a new car, or youth football camp. Try visualizing yourself enjoying the items you are focusing on. **Take the attitude that you are willing to keep going until you accomplish your goal.**

Shortly, we will discover how others have created their part-time-income ventures. For now, you're probably sitting on the fence, waiting for a sign of what your venture should be, or you may have the concept but have not yet moved forward with it.

Are you afraid to take action? If you don't act on your extra-income venture, ten years from now you'll still be wondering if you could have made it work. Look at your opportunity, now, and realize you must take action. Taking action is the key. Dabblers tend to keep dabbling but, without commitment, they will never reach that goal to actually start.

Karen loved to garden with vegetables, flowers, and herbs. She began to read more about flowers and herbs, and the next year, she planted lots of them. She was eating them, drying them for potpourri, and making little dried bouquets and wreaths. Within three years, Karen was engrossed in this form of gardening. She decorated her house, as well as the homes of her friends. People loved the items she made.

She decided to see if she had something people would buy. Karen worked feverishly for six months making wreaths, arrangements, potpourris, sachets, and pillows out of herbs and flowers. She rented a community building for a day and invited everyone she knew to her first herbal sale. Karen made over $7,000.00. This was just the beginning; she expanded into selling through mail order and published a newsletter, which generated a large following. This led into developing classes and then developing video-tape instructions.

Remember, no matter how great or how small your past success in life, the important thing is not where you've been but where you're going. After all, your past is not your potential. Your age, education, experience, and skills matter far less than your willingness to acknowledge your personal dreams. **Now commit yourself to making them come true.**

"You cannot teach a man anything. You can only help him discover it within himself." —Galileo

Patricia has a knack for making scrapbooks. She has made them for her family and friends. She realized that, with kids in high school and college, she had spare time and needed to earn some extra part-time income. So she decided to become a representative for Creative Memories; she was already using their products. Just by word-of-mouth and sharing her book samples, she has been making scrapbooks for all occasions. This is a great keepsake for elderly family members who may just have several boxes of old photos that need to be preserved. Patricia contacts the sons or daughters and interviews them. She then comes up with a script and a timeline and gets a feel for the person and his or her family. Many times, these older photos will need to be scanned and placed into a computer program. She then starts the book. She can give a password to family members, and they can watch the progress and give Patricia additional information and comments, while the book is in progress. Depending on how creative you are, there are several online programs, or even Walgreens photo development, to let you make the photo books. The number of people who might be interested in this service is endless. Here's a s hort list:

- Youth sports books for individual players or a season in sports for the whole team. What a change this is from getting the end-of-season trophy. The team can then sign the book and give one to the coach.
- High school sports
- That special vacation that never seems to get into an album.
- The first prom
- Charity events, golf outings

- Birthdays, wedding anniversaries, first communions, bar mitzvahs
- That special family reunion or picnic

Even though you are having fun doing this part-time venture, be sure you keep track of the time involved in each book. You don't want to be working for free. You can set up a training program or call it "scrapping buddies" for individuals or parents that want to get involved in photo book making. They can pay you a flat fee, and you can share your shortcuts and creativity with them.

Amy had a special knack for sewing and, when her grandmother had a mastectomy due to breast cancer, she needed special clothing. She contacted her local American Cancer Society and found out they had special patterns for mastectomy patients. Amy decided she would do some sewing for her grandmother. This was very rewarding for her. She did some more research and found there was a big need for clothing for people with special needs. It was best to talk with the people who had disabilities to find out what kind of modifications to clothing would best suit them. In most cases, they wanted their clothing to be comfortable, easy to wash and easy to put on and take off. Amy advertised with brochures in retirement and personal-care homes, along with Arthritis, Cancer Society, and VA hospital support centers. Placing ads in related newsletters also increased her exposure. Once she was established and ready to expand she could also look to advertise in *The American Legion*, *Disabled Veterans*, and the *AARP* magazines. People with disabilities want to look good and feel good, so any quality items that can be provide for them will increase your success in your part-time income venture, if you choose to follow Amy's example.

Jeremy always enjoyed setting up his aquarium and watching his tropical fish. When his friends and relatives visited, they always commented on how clear the water was and how beautiful the fish were. One day, while sitting in his dentist's office, he noticed how the filtering system in the aquarium wasn't doing its job (in other words, the aquarium was dirty) Jeremy, not being one to hold back anything, mentioned to the dentist, once he was in the chair, how he could fix the aquarium. Would *you* say that when the dentist could be drilling any second? I don't think so, but Jeremy had the personality to pull it off, and that weekend, he was overhauling the aquarium. The dentist was overwhelmed with Jeremy's work and offered to pay him. Jeremy joked to take it off his bill on his next visit.

But for Jeremy, this was the beginning of an extra-income opportunity. He figured that if other medical and professional establishments had aquariums, they probably need cleaning also. He made up some brochures and passed them out (he provided "before and after" pictures). He promised to stop by every month to check on the aquarium and to be on call if there was a special need. Jeremy went one step further; he approached professional offices, daycare centers, nursing homes, and doctors' offices, suggesting to them how relaxing it would be for their clients to watch an aquarium while waiting to be seen. Naturally, he would then promote his service program. This proved to be time well spent. In fact, his business exploded, and Jeremy soon started to hire high school biology students to help clean and maintain the aquariums.

While looking at all the different income-producing ventures, so far, one of the key ingredients for their success is the people who started them. They established themselves as experts. You can do this, too. Get involved in community organizations. Marketing your business doesn't have to cost a lot. Join your local chamber of commerce to partake in community-wide marketing. Most organizations are always looking for guest speakers, become one. Write a newsletter, newspaper article, or e-book—whatever—but get your name out there.

If you wait until you are sure, you will never take off the training wheels. You must start. Don't wait for the perfect time or until you have all the bugs worked out of your part-time income venture. Sometimes, you just need to take the first step; as with training wheels, raise one higher than the other, or take one completely off, but you must keep peddling.

Let's look at Jane, who is somewhat of an expert with computer software. Jane needed some extra money, since she liked to travel and was living on a fixed income. She decided to set up an online, how-to training program. This would let people learn at their own pace, anytime and anywhere. The training is online, 24-7-365. She started off with some basic courses in computer use, encouraging people to become more computer literate. And she now offers advanced courses for Microsoft certifications. You can start this type of business. Even if you aren't the expert, surround yourself with talented people, and you do the advertising, coordinating the classes and collecting the money. Remember, treat your experts with respect and pay them well, and they will keep bringing in your paycheck. Once the classes are online, the hard work is done. Your experts will just need to be available to answer questions, which may be submitted by e-mail, texting, or by phone. You let the instructors set this up.

Guy was always on the lookout for a good deal. He was walking through a flea market one Saturday, and a vendor had a pickup truck full of dining canopies at a price to die for. Guy bought them all. But now, what was he going to do with them? At first, he thought he would set up a table at smaller flea markets and sell them one at a time, but while walking to his truck, he wiped his head. Yes, it was hot and sunny that day and an idea hit him: RENT-A-TENT. His part-time income opportunity would be renting tents (dining canopies) for parties, vendors at flea markets, garage sales. No one wants to fool with setup and takedown, or fold up, lug around, or store tents. At first,

Guy contacted people who advertised garage and yard sales. Then word spread of the benefits and the low price of his rental service, and the requests for his services were so great, he needed to look for places to buy more canopies. He also had to find some high school students to help him deliver and set up the tents. Taking action was all it took for Guy to start earning that extra income.

Steve was a college student, who was looking for a way to earn some extra income. He worked construction during the summer of his sophomore year, and his apartment complex had a hot tub that he enjoyed sitting in after a long, hot workday. One day, while relaxing in the tub with a cold beer, a large smile came to his face. He would rent hot tubs on his college campus. There was always a party going on. That is just what he did. The tubs were the soft hot tubs. They were lightweight and easy to transport. Steve priced them and could afford to purchase six. He also needed to rent a self-storage space. He had a trailer that he could pull behind his car. He was in business. Water was no problem, since the students either lived in fraternity houses or apartments. Steve said that the only problem was that he had to clean them after each use. He also collected the money upfront, and there was always a deposit required in case of damage. This concept would work well on, say, Valentine's Day. What a nice, romantic end of an evening. If you want to do as Steve did or take it a step further, let your mind wander. You could have a building divided into separate rooms that would contain hot tubs; the rooms could be themed, Hawaiian, western, winter wonderland, the love shack, etc. You could have nice lighting effects, with music playing for that theme. You're up-sell could be drinks and snacks for each theme. You could rent the tubs by the hour or the evening. If you allow alcohol, you must post cautions about using alcohol with hot tubs.

If you are a fix-it-up type of person, be on the lookout for used bicycles and lawnmowers. George was, and he repaired them and then resold them at a nice profit. Sometimes, he would put an ad in the paper to pick up old bikes and mowers. Searching on Craigslist or free list.com really allowed him to get some nice items. If you do as George did, once the word gets out about your ability to repair and refurbish bicycles and lawnmowers, you will have more business than you will know what to do with. George says to watch what you wish for, especially if you don't have a large storage place. Good luck with this one. To develop a good name for yourself, donate the fixed items to a local charity. This will make you feel good and will get you either more bikes and mowers or more buyers.

As you continue on your journey to earning extra income, remember what you need this money for: your new car, new drapes for the house, a vacation, and new school clothes for the kids…**Don't fall in to the old rut of saying, "I can't afford it." You should be saying, "*How* can I afford it?"**

I hope you have a good idea of what you may want your extra-income opportunity to be by now. Write a one- or two-page strategy of what your business will be and how you are going to implement it. Then, be committed to it, and start to execute it. Many people make the mistake of spending all of their time making the plan but never taking that first step. Remember, while your competition is thinking about how good their plan is, you need to be executing yours. *Speed of execution* has proven to be what separates business opportunities that are successful from those that are failures. Start now with what you have, expose it to the real world, and see what happens. Remember, you can perfect it as you go.

- Get your business opportunity into production at the very earliest opportunity. As soon as you have something you might think might be viable, test it out in the real world. Stop thinking and planning about it, and start to move on it.

- Be committed to it! The best way to perfect it is to get moving and let the process inform you how to fix it if it needs fixing. If you just fool around with it, don't expect to win with it.
- Perfect as you go. The problem with most people is that they either think forever about what they're going to do and don't do it, or they implement it immediately and never learn and improve on it. The whole point of moving on your extra-income opportunity is to see if your plan will work and if you find it needs more work. Take the feedback you receive from the real world and tweak your plan.

As Harry Truman once said, "**Imperfect action is better than perfect Inaction.**"

Susan's husband Robert loved to travel and take pictures and wanted to sell them to make some extra income. He tried to sell them in local shops and at craft shows. He was not having as much success as he would like to have. Susan's idea was to start an online art gallery. She contacted local artists in her community and, for a fee, scanned their photos or photos of their artwork and sculpture into her computer. She posted her site onto various auction websites, where people from around the world could bid on the art items. Susan is also looking into starting her own site using PayPal for payment. Once the site is established, she is going to sell advertising from local supply stores. Depending on your computer skills, set the auction up so the artist will be notified when the bidding is finished. Once the money is collected, the artist is responsible for mailing the artwork.

Big G spent a lot of his spare time on the Internet looking for the big deal. His friends were always asking him what he had found. G would spend much of his time on Craigslist or Free List, and he gained much fun from the hunt. One day, one of his friends asked him to see if he could locate free building bricks, since he was building a patio. Big G got right on it and, within three days, he located his friend a pickup-truck load for $100.00. This was a great deal. Big G thought he could do the searches for a small fee, or a percentage of what the deal or purchase price was. Once word got out, Big G had plenty of part-time business and was earning a comfortable income, while enjoying the thrill of the hunt. He is now trying to land some contracts with companies who may be looking for specialty tools. Big G shows us how, if you love doing something, the money will follow.

Then there was Patsy Lee. She would go to the cemetery and place flowers on the graves of family members several times during the year. While she makes her way from her car to the grave site, she passes many graves and notices something that bothers her. Many of the same graves she passes every visit either have no flowers or wreaths and some have old plastic flowers that have faded over time. She recognizes some of the names on the headstones and knows the extended family members. Patsy approaches them and explains that she knows they would like to have the gravesites looking good, and says she will be able to help them. The three main visits would be birthday, Christmas, and Easter. (Other dates could be requested.)

Patsy Lee would do one of these for the family members:

- For a flat rate, she will purchase flowers or wreaths and place them on the grave site (she has pictures of different arrangements and their costs).
- Family member purchase flowers or wreaths, and Patsy Lee will place them on the gravesite.

She gets all contracts signed for a year. Patsy says being friendly to her clients opens the doors. Being a very nice person, she sometimes even takes the elderly with her when she places the flowers. Many clients are from out of town, so she takes a picture of the grave site and sends them the picture—just as an added touch!

Inspiration comes from the strangest places. Adrienne's mom had been living with her for ten years to help her out with her children when, one day, she decided the kids were going to school and she was not needed any longer, and she wanted to move back to her home town. Adrienne was in no condition to pack up her mother's belongings, let alone drive the moving van. She looked in the local yellow pages for senior moving services. To her surprise, there were none. Adrienne had to do it herself. She learned firsthand that moving seniors was no easy task. There was more to it than just packing up items, loading them in a truck, and unloading. There were many reason seniors are relocating, including the death of a spouse, moving in with a son or daughter, going to an assisted-living center or a retirement home. This author learned firsthand how an insensitive family member could shatter another family member. My aunt died and my cousin was moving my uncle out of a large house into a smaller house. My aunt was a collector but, to my cousin, it was junk, so he backed up a dump truck and started to throw the items out the window, as my uncle watched his wife's possessions and his memories drift away. Adrienne learned that moving seniors needed a sensitive touch. It was more than just packing and moving. There was clearing, sorting, organizing, transporting, unpacking, conducting estate sales, antique appraisals, and donations, heirloom delivery, cleaning and getting the house ready for the next owner. One major item that is often overlooked is counseling the senior members. This is a large change in their lives and this could make them very uncomfortable.

Adrienne realized there was a need for this type of work, so she started the Senior Relocation Service. Realizing this service was a very tender responsibility and could be very traumatic for people who are leaving and grieving for the home they've lived in for most of their adult lives, she had to employ a different type of person. Regular movers pack the boxes and then unpack, take everything out of the box, and leave it on the floor. Adrienne's Senior Relocation Service does all of this, but then places everything where it is supposed to be, displaying family pictures on tables, making the beds, and even putting the remote on the chair armrest. This is more than just unpacking; it is resettling. Adrienne stresses treating each client as if it were your own grandparent. It is very important to involve the senior as much as possible in this process. You are more than just a mover; you can be considered a counselor and adviser. Why is this service needed? Many seniors' children are grown and working in their own careers and have families of their own and can't be on hand to help or, often times, are overwhelmed and say they can't do this and realize they need help.

SOMEONE WHO'S GOT WHAT YOU WANT IS OUT DOING WHAT YOU'RE NOT THINK ABOUT IT! NOW IS THE TIME TO START THAT EXTRA-INCOME VENTURE

If you haven't come up with your extra-income opportunity yet, you need to compile your list of ideas, review what you have already listed, and begin researching which ones are most viable. Brainstorm as many ideas as possible; try to surround yourself with many people who are like-minded (looking for extra income). This is the time to generate fresh, original, and creative ideas.

Let's look at Terry. He is a curber—yes; he drives through his community the day before the scheduled bulk trash pickup day and loads his truck up with discarded items. His search is twofold: metal to recycle and items like bookcases, old furniture, small kid's items, power tools, and discarded building materials. You are probably asking how he makes his extra income. He makes it several ways: he knows crafters who refinish and paint furniture and will pay him a few dollars for bringing them furniture. He takes some items like power tools to pawn shops. The metal and aluminum are recycled; other items are sold to flee market sellers and, believe it or not, many people seem to have a garage sale every month and are willing to purchase some items. Remember, they are not going to be paying you very much, since they are going to resell the items (you are working on volume). Much of this business is Terry loves the hunt. Sometimes, he finds items he sells on e-bay. His business has increased since he learned about the online free cycle Network and Craigslist free category where people post and advertise items they are giving away. Terry does give this warning: if you are not careful, you can pile up a lot of items in a hurry, so you must have a market to move the items. There truly are treasures from trash.

Edward works a similar part-time business. He searches the free cycle Network and Craigslist and shops at Big Lots, Ollie's Outlet, Gabriel Brothers, dollar stores, and other local bargain outlets. Ed finds items he knows could be marked up and sells them on E-bay and Amazon. (Know your market and season of the year.) He bought a box of first-edition Notre Dame Fighting Irish Trading Cards for $4.00 at Ollie's Outlet, and then at the dollar store, he found a CD of the Notre Dame Victory March for $1.00 for a total investment of $5.00. He listed this package on E-bay (remember, there are some diehard Fighting Irish football fans), and the auction brought him $22.00, or a $17.00, plus shipping, profit. Ed says, "Know your market and this could be a great part-time, fun business. Children's brand name wearing apparel is also a great seller. Ed advises us to buy low and sell high.

Sophie from Michigan started making decoupage purses (hand bags); these were very popular back in the 1970s. (The crafting term "Decoupage" is the art of embellishing an object by gluing pictures or shapes cut out of paper onto other items.) Well people are interested again; back in the day, people used flowers and cut card pictures and thin magazine paper. Now, Sophie uses scrapbooking papers and scrapbook decorations. She has found two niches that she specializes in:

- She takes her clients' vacation photos and arranges them either on purses or trunks (or small chests).
- Her largest markets are college and pro sports. Once she finds true fans, word will spread by mouth and one tailgating event will generate more orders than she can imagine.

Paul started to make homemade clocks, but he was by no means a wood worker. He went to the local arts and craft stores and bought the different wood kits and clock workings. He started by just painting and staining them. As he perfected his skills, he started to decoupage flowers on his clocks. This was very nice for little, old ladies. Paul soon found his love for soccer and sports paid off and, as with Sophie, his largest markets are youth sports, college, and pro sports. For example, for Penn State football, the clock is painted blue and white, with the Penn State logo. (The school must give permission for the logo use. One way to go about this is through the alumni association and donate a percentage of sales back to the school.)

Like Paul and Sophie, once you find true fans, word will spread by mouth, and one tailgating event will generate more orders than you can imagine. You can place the year a person graduated or the years they won the super bowl into the decoupage.

Sonya liked to decorate her house inside and out for the different holidays. She likes to fly different flags outside by the front door. It seemed like everyone had the same style of flags and the same Easter Bunny picture. She was pretty good with a sewing machine, and so, at first, she would make some unique but simple pictures. As her skills got better, she started to give the flags as presents and house-warming gifts. Word started to spread, and people started to contact her to make custom flags. Here are some uses for customized flags:

- Celebrating a birth of a child (stork holding a baby with length and weight)
- College graduation (school logo and son or daughter's name and date)
- Flags depicting the different grade-level teams. One school ordered twelve flags.
- Banners with the team name and the sponsor's name
- Retirement flags

Sonya started to sell her flags at local craft shows and is now thinking of making a web site to sell on line.

Tom and Joann are a young couple with young children, and it seems that they are always going to Chuckie Cheese for birthday parties. They thought it would be nice to offer parents something different. There idea was to rent a store-front and place several inflatable bouncers inside (The Bounce House). They also had a party room. At first, to save money, they would order pizza and have it delivered, but once the concept caught on and the parties were proving to be successful, they started to make their own pizza, hotdogs, popcorn, and drinks. It is up to the parents to bring the cake.

This concept proved to be so successful, they are thinking of renting a warehouse and putting in a climbing wall, inflatable sport bouncers—soccer-ball kick, basketball shoot, bungee racer, baseball throw (with radar); this area would be geared for the teenagers.

Christina liked to sew, but saw a need for embroidery, so this was a perfect fit; she would take her samples to different businesses, sporting teams, car clubs, motor cycle clubs, cheerleading teams—anyone she could think of that might want to take their clothes to the next level above screen printing. She kept her overhead down by working out of her living room. Her motto is: no job is too small. This generated a lot of interest. There are many people who want one of a kind, special logos, etc. Christina is thinking of buying a van and going to company picnics, youth sporting games, swim meets. She said any place there are people is an opportunity to personalize hats, shirts, pants, and jackets.

Calvina had a flair for drawing and writing clever sayings. Her Idea was to design cards and market them. Her twist on this was to contact clients and ask them how many cards they send a year and to whom. She would get a little background information on the person, and she would set up the cards for a year; the addresses would be printed and arraigned by months and delivered to the client. All the client needed to do was personalize and sign the card and drop it into the mail. As an added service, Calvina made a tickler file and would notify the client two weeks in advance when it was time to mail the card. The client list includes the very busy executive, the elderly, and the client who just has to outdo the card from the year before.

Bruce, a high school student, wanted to work in an electronics store. He could not find a part-time job. He was getting discouraged, but came up with an idea to set up people's electronics, including DVD players, TV's, and computers, networking everything together.

He had a knack for details; he would tie the cables together and arrange them in a very orderly manner. He also had patience and would explain to his clients how to operate the individual appliances. One drawback was his age, and many people were afraid to let a teenager in their house. So, once he established himself, he made up tri-fold flyers with pictures and references from his clients. Word of mouth was his best advertisement.

Mason was helping his grandmother clean out the storage shed when he came across two boxes of old VHS tapes; it looked like no one had looked at them for several years. His grandmother was getting up in age, so he decided he would transfer the tapes to DVDs for easier viewing. After doing some Internet research, he found a machine for around $200.00 that would let him transfer the movies. Since it was for his grandmother, his father bought the machine. On his grandmother's birthday, the family was in for a big treat. You guessed it; they all got to view the old movies. Mason soon decided this could be a good part-time business. He made up some flyers and passed them out to the neighbors and left some at the local retirement home. The response was overwhelming. He is now making CDs of people's favorite music, combining songs from different CDs, so the people can listen to just the songs they like.

Jo Jo liked to walk. She was heavy, and walking was her way to control her weight. She was upbeat and very friendly, and people liked being around her. Her friends started to see how she was losing her weight and wanted to start walking with her. Some of them started but soon stopped, so Jo Jo decided to start charging $1.00 a day to walk with her. She realized that, if people paid, they would stick with the program, and they did. It was all for fun, and since Jo also liked to cook, she used the money and baked some healthy snacks and shared them with her walking friends. She decided to start a newsletter on walking and diet control. She developed menus and a form to track the miles. Word spread on how much fun the ladies were having and how much success they were having in losing weight. The ladies soon wanted to start jogging, and some even wanted to train for a 5K race. Jo started to give talks and even made some training programs. She turned a fun walking program into "Average Jo's," a workout-training program. If you give the people what they want, they, in turn, will give you what you want: fame and fortune.

Gram was a runner, and he also knew where to get a good buy on his running shoes. His running buddies always had something to say about his new shoes. What they didn't know was that he wasn't paying full price for them. One day, when he was at the factory outlet (not the stores that say they are the factory outlets), he loaded up his car trunk and headed for home. His first stop was a local watering hole, where many of his buddies went after the Saturday long run. He opened up his trunk and said, "Hey guys, look at what I have for you—a great shoe at a great price." They were his friends, so he only made a few dollars on each pair he sold. But selling enough added up, and Gram never used his own money to buy his shoes again. He did the same thing for baseball and soccer spikes; then he tried basketball and golf shoes. He would find a good location and not try to make a killing. Remember; when you help enough people get what they want, you will get what you want. There was one customer who wanted in on Gram's deal. He saw a good thing and just wanted to market basketball shoes. Gram made him a deal where Gram would sell him the shoes at only $1.00 over his cost. This deal made him a nice, little, part-time income for doing next to nothing.

Think what other items you could use this concept with.

- Sunglasses
- Baseball hats
- Golf balls

Stan was a specialist with kitchen knives. He would go to bowling lanes, local fraternal clubs, anywhere a large group of people gathered. He would talk to the owner and either set up a deal, where the owner would get a free set of whatever he was selling, or he sometimes convinced the owner or club president that it would be a good service to provide to their customers or club members.

Then there was Ski. Several times a year, he would rent a U-Haul truck and go to the candy outlet at Easter time. He would load up on premade Easter baskets and large chocolate bunnies. He would park outside the gate of the steel mill, where he sold out his supply every time. It would be hard for the parents to pass up a good deal without any shopping headaches. The other time he did well was Valentine's Day, when he sold flowers and boxed candy.

Billy used the same concept, but he would get pots and pans, and any other type of kitchen item, including can openers, toasters, and microwaves. Billy sold out several times, and then he would move the location. You will find out it is very hard for people to pass on what they perceive to be a deal.

What other items, bought at discount would work this way?

Tools, hanging plants for Mother's Day, Frozen Turkeys for Thanksgiving, Hams for Easter, Cases of soda pop, and bags of potato chips—will all sell easily. And how about $5.00 or $10.00 watches? Look at your local area and brainstorm what you think people will buy on impulse.

Kari and Josh lived in the country but had access to a great location next to a highly traveled road. A friend of the family had several large cornfields that he would harvest when the corn was ripe and ready to pick. As with any crop, not all the vegetables ripen at the same time, but for Sam to go back in and pick the remaining corn was too time-consuming and expensive. Sam would let Kari and Josh go through the fields and collect the remaining corn, and they would take it to their roadside stand next to the highly traveled road and, during the summer, they sold many dozens of ears of corn. In the fall, they would sell pumpkins and apples.

Like Sonya, Richard had a flair for design and soon decided to personalize his homemade special-occasion signs. He got his idea from seeing a stork in his neighbor's front yard, announcing the birth of their baby girl. Richard wanted to do something different, so he had a local high school art teacher design him some pictures like the Grim Reaper for over-the-hill parties and, for birthdays, a large cake with candles and a place on the front for the age. One fun card says, "Lordy, Lordy look who turned 40." He uses an overhead projector or LCD projector to enlarge the picture and then paints it on plywood. He then personalizes the design with the person's name, birthday, birth, super bowl, anniversary, or graduation. Richard rents his signs by the day, three days or for a whole week. His prices range from $25.00 a day to $35.00 for three days, and $50.00 per week. This price includes delivery, setup, and take down.

You can do the same thing. Get some pictures from children's coloring books; they are usually simple and easy to enlarge. You should have an inventory of about twenty-five items. Once you get your business going, you will know what to stock (it is very important to keep a fresh coat of paint on your signs). **I would also advise you to put a little sign on the bottom, so other people will know how to contact you.** Your special-occasion sign business will spread by word-of-mouth to start, but you will also need to advertise with flyers. One great place to put your flyers is in OBGYNs' offices. You may want to wholesale the signs or sub-contract with a party store. Richard says this is a fun business but suggests you get a signed rental contract, as some people like to keep the signs. If it is a popular sign like a super-bowl champion Pittsburgh Steeler player, other people may want to take it, so you may want to place a cable lock around it.

James was a teacher and a part-time baker. His specialty was rolls for every major holiday. He would take orders for dozens of his rolls. When he first started, he made samples and gave them away. Almost everyone who sampled his rolls made an order. It became a tradition in the local area; you had to have James' rolls on your table. He did the same thing with his crab cakes. This part-time venture turned into a full-time business, once he retired. He bought himself a trailer and worked the local fairs and events. If you do something similar, James cautions that you must follow health regulations.

Aaron liked to eat hot nuts and realized there were probably many others who would like hot nuts, so he decided to open up a vending cart, specializing in "Hot Nuts." He did his research and located suppliers for the nuts. With this business, he had to set it up where people had the chance to sample the nuts. He decided to make his stand a little different: his customers would have to sample the different nuts, from the mild to the very hot. This kept people at his stand longer and attracted a lot of viewers, which proved good for business. Aaron had four really hot nuts and made the customers sign a release before they sampled the nuts. This just added a little mystique to the sampling. His primary business includes fairs, arts and crafts shows, street-rod shows, motorcycle shows, and at Christmas, he rents a space in the mall. At this time, he is looking to set up a web site, so he can do mail order.

Phil, a successful high school coach, decided there were so many parents that thought their children had athletic ability that he developed programs that were general and sport-specific (The Training Room). His programs are developmentally sound, where he works on general fitness and sport-specific skills, like videoing and analyzing the baseball swing, stretching for general and sport-specific fitness, proper breathing techniques, visual tracking skills, weight lifting, Plyometrics, speed, and aerobic conditioning. His key to developing and maintaining the program is that he makes it fun. Phil states that there are so many fun, engaging, skill-enhancing games that motivate his athletes that they want to keep coming back. The parents are happy, because their athletes are improving with their sport skills and everyone leaves as a winner. Phil doesn't recommend going into a venture like this just for the money; making sound choices for the athletes should be in the forefront for all your decisions. Remember, if you help enough people get what they want, you will get what you want.

Adam is a cart vender. He purchased a snow-cone cart, which he named "The Slush Puppy." He started out doing children's birthday parties. He charges a flat rate, and the kids get to eat as many slush puppies as they want. The parents love it, since they don't have to deal with the mess. He has expanded into other areas, such as corporate company picnics, fairs, school PTA events, construction sites, youth sporting events, and social festivals. There are several types of vending carts.

- Push
- Towable
- Peddle
- Hot
- Cold

There are plain carts, custom carts, themed carts, food carts, beverage carts, sunglasses carts, etc., from which you can sell shaved ice, peanuts, flowers, coffee, ice cream (hand dipped or on a stick). Some of the major vends from carts are hot dogs, snow cones, Italian Ice, pretzels, cotton candy, popcorn, soft drinks, cold sandwiches, sun glasses, and then there is a little machine called Lil'Orbits, where your customers can actually watch their mini-donuts being cooked.

Adam says to start with an item you really enjoy working with. Many people own several carts and pay operators to work them in different locations. He operates different carts for different seasons. Hot sausage carts are growing in popularity. Who can resist that aroma? He is also thinking of renting out the carts to other entrepreneurs or little-league baseball teams.

Mark was traveling in Mexico and came across street vendors selling seasoned grilled corn on the cob. This was food cart vending at its finest. Be the first in your area to offer Mexican Street Corn at street fairs, festivals, craft and auto shows. Depending on the seasoning used you will have different flavors. Here are just a few variations Thai,

Italian, Indian, and Mexican. If you don't want to grill the corn, it could also be prepared in a 500 degree oven. I strongly suggest the grilling. This will let people see their corn being prepared and as we have learned people are very visual let alone the aroma that will be given off. Please go to www.parttimeincomeenterprise.com to download some fine street corn recipes.

Regina took hair and nail classes, but she didn't want to be tied down to sitting in a shop for eight hours a day, so she went mobile. She had a very nice van, and her boyfriend outfitted it for her, and she was in business. (It is very important to have a good exhaust fan.) The flexibility and skilled work she offered her clients was her selling point. She is now thinking about franchising her concept.

Brian and Mary Jo started a tree-pruning and cutting service; they took a tree-care class at a community college, and Brian worked one summer for a tree-cutting company. When they went into business, they soon found that most people did not want the wood, and it was theirs, just for the taking. They had a large back yard and, after splitting the wood, they stacked it, and in the Fall, they were ready to load the truck. They had another stream of part-time income.

Erica was a fan of *Home and Garden* TV and became interested in patios and walkways. She took a class at a local home and garden store and fell in love with the brick and stonework. It was hard work, but she loved it and, after she did some free jobs for family and friends, she was ready. She put together her portfolio of pictures and references, and her part-time-income opportunities soon turned into a full-time business.

Ronda loved gardening and had a two-acre plot of land not far from her home. She advertised garden plots for rent. It didn't take long for all the plots to be rented. She had it all plowed up as part of the service. She soon found out that many people did not know the first thing about planting and taking care of a garden plot. With some quick thinking, she offered (for a price) to help them get the soil ready and setting out of the plants. This was just the beginning; when the weather turned hot, many people did not want to come and weed their garden. This was another area in which some people were willing to pay for help. Some of the garden plots produced much more produce than the owners could use. Ronda had her husband build a vegetable stand, and their daughter worked as a sales person, selling the extra vegetables. The profits, after her hourly rate, were divided among the people that provided the produce. This was a win-win for all involved. With just a little planning and quick thinking, Ronda turned her spare time and vacant land into a profitable, part-time, income-producing venture.

Don was in the Air Force and learned how to polish floors. He became an expert with the buffer and earned considerable extra money by contracting himself out as a floor technician. Don started with auto parts stores, and then added some grocery stores. He was able to alternate work nights, so he could schedule all his jobs on a two-week rotation. He is debating now whether or not to expand. This is always a hard decision to make. Will he be able to find and train someone who is responsible enough to do a quality job, since Don's name will be on the line? Can workers be bonded? Many storeowners will not let contractors in unless they are bonded, due to the possibilities of theft. Don is also looking at starting a training program for floor technicians. He feels there is enough part-time work out there for quality workers (plus, he will be able to use his apprentices to work on some of his contracts).

Jan and Sharon were friends who liked to sew and read Harlequin Romance books. They both had quite a collection of old sewing patterns and paperback books. They decided to clean up, since they hadn't used the patterns or looked at the books for several years. They decided to see if they could earn some extra income. A garage sale was ruled out, since most people would not realize the value of the vintage items. The ladies opened an Etsy.com account. Their advice is to list what you are selling in the name of your shop; this way, when people are searching for your key items, they will be directed to your shop. Once you sell your items, and if you still like this type of part-time work, check with your friends and see if you can list their unwanted items.

Remember Margo the bead jewelry maker? She is now considering opening an Etsy account to sell her one-of-a-kind creations.

Bobby has been collecting music cassettes and CDs for quite awhile; he finally realized he only listens to a few of them. They were taking up way to much room in his house. He decided to open up an Amazon selling account, and soon found out that his unwanted collection of music was on many people's buy list. It didn't take him long to realize there was money to be made on Amazon.

EBAY is another place to sell your merchandise. Edward is a garage-sale junkie and can't pass up a deal; he goes out early and makes some really great buys, then comes back to his house and lists them on EBAY. Edward advises to cross-list the items. For example, you have this old pearl pin. You should list it as "pearl brooch, brooch, pin, jewelry." By using this method you will ensure more bidders can find it. When listing your items, take uncluttered pictures on a plain white backdrop; list the item at the lowest price you'll accept. Setting an unrealistic price will just turn buyers off. You can specialize in collectables or just sell regular items you feel people will buy. Just be honest with the condition of the items. Nothing will ruin your business as quickly as bad reviews. Try to keep it fun and don't stress out if you don't sell all the items at a large profit. Small profits will all add up to a big payday by the end of the month. And when you do net the big sale, it will all be worth it. You will be surprised to find there are people out there for every niche market.

Ebony uses her E-bay selling skills not only to sell her stuff/junk. (You would be surprised what some people will buy and what they will pay for it). Ebony will check out the newspaper ads and contact people who are scheduled to have garage or yard sales. She tries to work a deal for items she feels she could sell for a good price. Ebony either buys it direct or will work on a commission basis. She also goes to thrift stores and looks for items she knows she can sell. When selling on E-bay having a nice picture really helps your sales. People are visual and like to see what they are buying. Ebony will also go to a person's house and take pictures of their items and post them on E-bay for them once the sale is complete. It is the responsibility of the items owners to mail it out.

Once you start networking you will find out many people have lots of stuff but don't have the time or the skills to list and follow it on E-bay. So Ebony is their go to person. You could establish yourself as a professional E-bay seller that specializes in only certain items, like specialty glass, sport cards, Christmas ornaments, ceramics, bird pictures, costume jewelry, model trains, and children clothes. Any niche you may have an interest in and can find a ready supply of inventory will surely put some extra money in your pocket.

Yahoo Store: This business is very similar to E-bay in the sense that it's a very large-sized marketplace but more similar to a store in the true sense of the word. It is like having your own retail outlet but without the hassles of rent, employees, utilities and all the other expenses of a traditional brick-and-mortar store.

The really good thing is that it can be as hands-on or as hands-off as you want it to be because of companies called drop-shippers, which can do most of the work for you. In fact, you don't even pay for the inventory until you make a sale. Now that is really fantastic and almost unheard of in retail.

Most people think the hard part of this business would be creating your virtual store, but nothing could be further from the truth. Yahoo! Has made the templates and wizards so easy a third grader can do it!

The best way to ensure your success is to do your homework and research to find what products people most want to buy. You need to find a niche. Once again, start with things you enjoy. For example let's say you love fishing. What products do fishing folks want to buy most? (Or get even more specific, like, what are bass fishermen looking to buy?)

Then the task is to find the right source of these products so you can carry them in your Yahoo! Store. In most cases, you will be able to pull pictures and product descriptions directly from your sources and plug them right into your store.

As you can see, this business requires a little bit more upfront work, but once it's done it can be maintained with very little regular input on your part.

Are you ready to start making your part-time income on the internet now?

Patsy, an avid gardener, decided he was tired of buying plant food when he could make his own for a lot less. He realized that, even if he used good compost, he needed to feed his plants. House plants need fertilizer more than those in the garden. If you want the best looking and yielding plants, you need to provide them with extra food.

Patsy's simple homemade formula is to use a tablespoon of Epsom salts, a teaspoon of baking soda, and a quarter teaspoon of ammonia. He mixes it all together, then adds a half-gallon of warm water and stirs until dissolved. He adds another gallon of water and uses this to water his plants once a month.

His advice for acid-loving plants like blueberries, strawberries, or azaleas, is going right to the source: vinegar. Use the above solution and add a couple of teaspoons of vinegar, or simply use a half-cup of vinegar to a gallon of water, and pour it on the ground around the plants. Don't use it directly on the foliage, as it will burn and may kill the plants. For houseplants, only use a tablespoon of apple cider vinegar to a gallon of water. Not only does vinegar lower the Ph, it adds potassium and around fifty trace minerals.

To advertise his plant food, Patsy placed a one-page flyer with tear-off tabs on local bulletin boards; he also sent them to his friends who lived in different towns and states. He also runs small ads in newspapers and some magazines, advertising how to make homemade plant food for a whole lot less money. His asking price is $1.00 and a self-addressed, stamped envelope. He mails customers the information and, as a bonus, he gives this other homemade fertilizer formula:

- 1 tbs Epsom salts
- 1 tsp bicarbonate of soda
- ½ tsp saltpeter
- ¼ tsp household ammonia
- ½ gallon warm water
- Mix it all together and use sparingly.

Patsy says making your own plant food makes sense when you look at the cost of a small box of granules or small bottle of liquid plant fertilizer.

What special information or recipe do you have that you could sell?

Sandy did it with her recipe for "Homemade Root Beer Soda Pop." Here it is. Get ready, the recipe makes one gallon.

Ingredients:
- 2 cups sugar
- 1 teaspoon yeast
- 2 tablespoons root-beer extract

Easy Step–By-Step Directions:

Step 1   Put all ingredients in a clean gallon jug, with about a quart of very warm *(not hot)* water.

Step 2   Stir until ingredients are well mixed.
Finish filling the jug with warm water.

Step 3   Let stand six hours, lightly covered *(so the lid is not sealed)*.
               At the end of the six hours, screw lid on and refrigerate.

Step 4   Enjoy!

Sandy also went one step further and set up at local craft fairs, where she offered free taste samples of her Homemade Root Beer. Once the people marveled at the taste, she would then sell them the recipe for $1.00. She had the recipe printed on themed paper, so it looked like an old family recipe, which adds to the authenticity of the formula.

Robert, a science teacher, really had dynamic lessons, so he and his wife decided to put together Science Camps during the summer. The camps were one week long and were geared for elementary and middle-school aged students. The camps were hands-on and action packed. They were so successful there were waiting lists. When Robert retired, he developed one day, half-day, two-hour, and one-hour, action-packed, hands-on demonstrations (lessons). Most of the time, the school PTAs would sponsor the program and pay the fees. Robert and his wife enjoyed making the presentations and the extra income they produced.

Allison, another teacher, enjoyed making bulletin boards and helping students design Science Fair Backboards. She turned this skill into a part-time venture. The apartment complex where she lived had a recreation center, and she offered classes and hands-on help for science-fair backboards. Students would come with their data, and Allison would help them make it visually appealing. She expanded this to making bulletin boards. Teachers would contact her with the concept, and Allison would cut the letters and design the bulletin board. The teacher would just need to attach it to the wall. Allison would take pictures and keep them in a three-ring binder to advertise her work.

Clint collects aluminum beer and soda pop cans and recycles them at the local recycling center, and then buys his grandson savings bonds.

David collects all types of metals and hauls them to the local scrap yard.

Bagley cleans garages for a small, flat fee and gets to keep all the throw- a-way items. He then sells them in thrift shops, flea markets, or garage sales.

Ken, a swim coach, teaches basic swim classes at the local wellness center and, during the summer, at several outdoor recreation centers. Most centers let him use the pools for free, since he provides a service for their members. He does charge a small fee for the lessons, and this is how he makes his part-time income.

Diane was an accomplished piano player and decided she would like to teach piano to earn her extra income. She soon discovered that there were many people who were interested in learning how to play a musical instrument. Diane had many friends who were interested in earning extra income. So she worked deals with the instructors to earn a small finder's fee for everyone she referred. This proved to be an easy way to earn a little extra, part-time income.

Jeff belongs to a hunt club and, between him and the other members; they shoot more deer than they can eat. Jeff and the guys like to eat deer jerky. Jeff decided he would start making jerky and sell it as his part-time-income venture. He developed a special blend of seasoning and started with several food dehydrators. It didn't take him long to realize he needed to invest in larger dehydrators. Jeff started by selling the jerky to friends and family, but word soon spread, and some of the local stores wanted to carry the jerky. Jeff is thinking of starting a mail-order business. His only concern now is whether he will be able to find enough meat to keep up with the demand.

John loved the smell of homemade bread. He loved to bake bread and, most of all; he liked to eat the bread. John liked to make special breads to which he added berries; he added nuts and even olives. The excitement of the different breads was overwhelming. John set up home parties where the guests would provide the main dish, and John would provide the bread and spreads. This soon developed into John taking orders and developing regular clients. Holidays were especially busy times for Strictly Bread.

Bill was an insurance salesman, but when he was talking to his clients, they always seemed concerned about their retirement. So Bill put together a team of specialists who would put together a plan for his clients. This started as a basic road map into retirement. Once the clients saw where they were at the present time, they could start to work the plan. Bill soon started to make more money from the retirement program than from his insurance sales. Specialized knowledge and knowing how to put together a quality team is the key to this successful venture.

Dan is an engineer and likes to ski, so he made himself available to ski resorts to inspect their ski lifts. He did this for a reduced fee and free skiing. This also turned in to a vacation for his family.

Dave is a veterinarian and exchanges his services of taking care of the family pets for Philip, a lawyer who, in turn, looks over any legal forms Dave needs in his business, this form of bartering doesn't put ready cash in Dave's pocket but it saves him money in the long run.

What other professional skills, can you think of where people can exchange their expertise? Here are just a few: brick layers, carpet installers, CPAs, computer experts, photographers, and the list goes on.

What special skill do you have that you can barter with?

Shaun has a knack for spotting a need. He realized every business, no matter how small or large, should have an online presence. This presence can be just an online business card telling people who they are and what they do, how to find /contact them or find out more information. Shawn says "A business without a sign is a sign of No Business". In this case the sign is their online presence.

Shawn did not have any design or programming skills to create and/ or maintain simple one page websites let alone a full-fledged e-commerce site. He did however know several high school and college students who had the skills to create the sites. He had his student professionals make him a website where he explained what he could provide along with sample pages. Shaun had to start beating the pavement contacting every business he could think of. Beauty shops, pizza shops, Boy and Girl Scout troops, lawn services businesses gutter cleaners, home handy men, plumbers, painters, pet groomers, massage therapists, personal trainers, auto detailers etc. When lining up the programming jobs he also offered a secure domain name and hosting service. (He used Go Daddy)

*There are several companies. For example, www.ipage.com and www.1and1.com that offer you web sites but many times they want to sell you marketing plans, per click etc. Be cautious on their many up sales. Also many sites even though they say no experience is needed to make your home page. You must have an idea of what you are doing. Also be sure it is easy to contact them if you need help it can become very frustrating and time consuming to make what they say is a simple web site.

Shaun charged a fair price and worked on volume and paid his workers (independent contractors) a price they were happy with. He also branched out with a special service using the same students as the go to persons for setting up different programs like Skype; surround sound systems, computer networks, printers, general TV remote programs, or DVD players. One of the most popular things his student reps did was to leave the (usually older folks) a detailed step by step instruction information sheet to follow along with the phone number for their internet provider and cable company, just in case the internet would go down and they need a new signal sent. Anyway you can help make the technology challenged person's life easier will put dollars in your pocket.

Justice, a high school student, started to sell books on Amazon at such a young age he really made some very good connections getting close out books. I mean lots of books in very good condition. Even though I had a good relationship with Justice he never revealed where the books came from. Some things are best unanswered. I can tell you he sold an amazing number of books.

Then there was Mark. He also sold books on Amazon but he specialized in books where he could make really good money. (Do to shipping charges sometime you are making money even if you only sell the book for one penny) Mark wanted to make a good profit on the books he sold. He did not like to carry a large inventory. When he went shopping for books his niche was college books and rare out of date books. Mark used his smart phone and when he came across a book he thought might be a good buy he would search to see what it was selling for and then make his decision. This worked for Mark. Once again you must know your audience. You might want to specialize in "how to" books, woodworking, gardening, or specialty foods. Do your Google search and see what people are looking for and fill that need (word tracker).

Emily has a website and a blog. She was always looking for a simple way to generate extra part-time income without much effort. She discovered Infolinks- In Text Advertising. This is where the infolinks program intelligently scans your web pages or blog and converts carefully selected key words into cost-per click (CPC) in text ads. This double underline hyperlink leads to highly relevant advertiser content. You cannot see the ads until the reader moves their mouse over the double underline words and clicks. Emily says the good news is you get paid every time a visitor clicks on the in text ad Infolinks is easy to set up in a matter of minutes. You may be asking will the infolinks ads be relevant to your site's content. Yes, by using their proprietary algorithms when scanning your pages they select your key words. This is a free way to generate extra money.

To learn more about in text advertising you can go to Barnesandnoble. com and get the guide book entitled "The Hidden Treasure in Your Website" by Infolinks' CMO Tomer Treves.

Many people are using You tube to promote and grow their businesses. Frank is a Life Insurance salesman and uses You tube as part of his marketing. He directs people to his You tube channel where he asks for only <u>TWO minutes</u> of their time and he will show them how to save 30% in premiums in their life insurance. Even on his website he has a link to his You tube channel. His business card has a link to You tube. Once people view the You tube video they feel more comfortable calling to set up an appointment. Frank says don't try to sell anything in the video. Just use it to get people to call for more information.

If you have a product or a program to sell start posting videos on You tube. By increasing your presence, you are increasing awareness and positioning yourself as an authority. Direct your viewers to some free sites where they can get more information about what you are an expert on. You can also have a membership based site where you can sell your products such as information, books, e-books, CD's, electronic equipment. On this site list other items that are related to your niche (using affiliate marketing)

Here is how Ike used You tube. Ike makes custom wooden baseball bats. In his videos he talks about the wood he uses, where it comes from, how it's selected, different weights, etc. By sharing this information he becomes a self proclaimed expert. He also shares batting tips, strength training programs, visual training etc. His videos show him making the bats and explaining why and how he does it. On his web site he advertises balls, gloves, hats, etc using affiliate marketing which brings in a little extra money. Some of the bats are not up to the strict baseball standards. They can be used in kid's bed rooms and personalized with their names cut out using a band saw. Bats can be personalized with season records, state championships, etc. Ike has players in professional, minor league and collegiate baseball using his bats. Ike says "know your business cycles". When he is making his You tube videos winter will be slow so he talks about bats as gifts and how he can personalize them. Spring and summer will be prime time for videos due to baseball season.

Ideally the real money is made when you become a member in the You tube's partner program. This program provides creators with resources and opportunities to improve their skills, build larger audiences – relationships, and earn more money through the placement of relevant ads inside or near the video. You earn a share of the revenue that is generated when the video is viewed. You really must have a large audience to make real money.

Here is a little different part-time income opportunity e-Juror #3 makes either $5.00 or $10.00 depending on the length of the case. You will see the amount to be paid at the top of each case. What is e-Jury? E-Jury provides an attorney the opportunity to "pre-try" the case before it goes to trial in front of an actual jury at the courthouse. Usually 50 e-Jurors are used to gather input to help the attorney find strengths and weaknesses in the evidence, learn public attitudes, etc. Once you sign up www.ejury.com you will be notified by e-mail that a new case has been posted. You, the e-Juror, go to the e-Jury web site, logs in and reviews the facts and answers the questions. Then clicks a submit verdict button upon completion.

You will be paid via Pay Pal. You certainly won't get rich serving as an e-Juror, you will earn a little spending money and have some fun, and provide a needed service. Go to www.ejury.com to learn more about how it works and the qualifications for actual e-Jury service. There are no charges or costs for signing up to be an e-Juror. There is also no guarantee that there will be cases for you to complete once you sign up. Cases are assigned based upon availability from attorneys, where you live, and your demographic details. E-Jurors living in major metropolitan areas receive more cases for participation than jurors living in rural areas.

Are you an expert or know a lot about a certain field or subject? If so, you can get paid to share this information. Angela is listed as a Homework Expert in her area of specialization. There are literally thousands of questions asked. She thought she would make a few dollars. She is doing way better than she ever expected. Here is how it works. People asking questions offer to pay a certain amount for their answer. A new expert will earn 25% of what a customer is offering to pay for the answer. A stage 4 expert will earn up to 50%. A positive rating for your answer must be received.

There are over 20 million customers using www.justanswer.com . So there is a need for your expert advice. Why would you like to be listed as an expert?

- Earn money for your knowledge
- Help others solve their problems
- It's fun
- Flexible hours (it's open 24/7/365)
- You can learn from other experts

When you go to www.justanswer.com you will need to fill out an application and have your credentials verified. This will be by different categories. Here is only a sample of expert categories – fire arms repair, parenting, power point/ presentations, antiques, motorcycle repair, social security, dog training, bankruptcy law, cat veterinary, plumbing etc.. There are 100's of categories. If you are an expert but don't see your category you can even start a new category. As a founding expert for a new category you won't need credentials just yet. So go to www. justanswers.com now to start earning your expert part-time income.

Remember Patsy and his plant food recipe and Sandy and her homemade root beer recipe. Well they found out that selling recipes using the internet can be a gold mine. People can down load the recipe and receive it instantly, or you can e-mail it to them. This will save you the cost of a first class stamp and envelope. You can fax the recipe if you can fit it on one page. In most cases it is cheaper than a first class stamp since it usually is less than one minute.

Once you find some really good recipes for special dishes – seafood, cookies, grilling etc. get them listed on the internet. People are always surfing for gourmet recipes and you can e-mail it to them and they can be cooking in less than an hour. Using pay pal, www.paypal.com is a convenient way to take payment.

Remember; only sell one recipe at a time. This will keep your cost down and keep people coming back to your site. It is also good if you can put a little bit of history to your recipe. This will bring in the social aspects and as we know in selling and sharing, people like to connect.

The simplest website to set up is a one page direct sales letter. It's just ONE page explaining how a given product is going to improve the prospects' life. Traffic is driven to the website where the person either buys or leaves, or in some instances joins a list **example** (special cookie recipe of the month club) cost $10.00. You then e-mail them a cookie recipe every month. Your cost is ZERO Dollars. You could also encourage your members to send in one of their favorite cookie recipes. Compile them giving credit to the submitter and back end the sale of an e-book giving your submitters a reduced price. Once again your out of pocket cost is ZERO dollars. Just your time! One good thing about selling recipes and information on the internet is that your start up costs is low, and you can experiment with different types of information.

Amy was looking for a way to earn some extra income. While searching the Internet, she came across gazelle.com, where you can recycle electronics for cash. She started with a few items she had at home, including cell phones, a LCD monitor, and some old 35 mm camera lenses. It worked just like they said, so Amy decided she would contact her friends and see what they had laying around the house (she approached them on being environmentally responsible). They were eager to have someone take their unwanted items off of their hands. This worked for a while and, now, Amy is expanding her searches to thrift stores, and she is placing containers at local grocery stores, where people can drop off their used and unwanted items.

Mike is trained as a health and physical education teacher but, due to tough budget times, he could not find a regular teaching position. He decided to go out on his own. He developed a training program geared for the pre-school-age child. The program is typically offered on a weekly basis in four ongoing nine-week terms, following a regular public school timeline. The classes include a class orientation and safety session, lifetime fitness and health information section, movement lessons, and a review period. This is a well planned out program. Mike goes to private preschools and daycare centers on a rotating schedule. Follow-up materials are provided for home use. This program works in two ways: The schools pay for the program and provide it to the parents and students as an extra add-on program. Or Mike provides forms, and the parents that are interested contract with Mike, and their kids meet him when he comes to their daycare. However he chooses to work it, this class becomes the highlight of each child's week.

Debra does something a little differently with her program; she outfitted a recycled school bus into a mobile gym for preschoolers; the emphasis is on gymnastic skills. She established a route and travels to the local preschools.

Scott, a personal trainer, uses the same concept, but his bus has a changing area, free weights, some machines, and an aerobic area. For convenience, Scott pulls up to his client's driveways or meets them at their workplace.

What other themes can you take on the road?

- Computer classes
- Art classes
- Video gaming
- Beauty shop (spa) for young girls
- Cooking class
- Beading
- Sewing classes where the bus is outfitted with several sewing Machines and cutout area

Todd is a police officer who moonlights as security for special concert events; he gets paid and also gets to hear the concert. He also instructs safety and self-defense classes.

Beth just got a new puppy and read books on how to train it. It seemed she had an incredible knack for teaching the puppy. She enjoyed this bonding with the animal so much that she decided to work with some of her friends' dogs. She met with such positive success; she decided to charge a small fee to earn her extra income.

Now, let's look at Kim, a high school student, who took telecommunications as a class. She became quite an expert with the video camera and developed her interviewing skills. Kim decided she wanted to use her skills to earn extra income. She approached local bands and business owners and explained to them how having videos to use in their advertising would increase their bottom line. She went on the premise that everyone would like to be on film, and she effectively used the old adage that "a picture is worth a 1,000 words." She was right. The videos of the band were posted on their web site and highlights were used to make a promo disk; copies were then made for them to hand out to prospective clients. Real estate brokers, landscape and garden centers, car sales people, and home improvement companies are just a few that took advantage of Kim's skills and low price. Their videos showed samples of their projects. The videos could also be used as instruction programs; for example, a real estate sales person could make a video on how to stage a house before an open house.

Kim is now looking into the area of high school sports with every athlete trying to get into college with a scholarship, so she figures they will need a highlight video. She plans on interviewing the athlete, show his or her stats, show them working out in the weight room, and interview the coach. Then she will edit and put in the highlight video clips. This would also make a great memory tape for the family.

The ideas are endless, and Kim has plans to make videos for high school seniors to send in with their collage applications (something to get the committee's attention).

How about filming members of families to develop family histories? The older members especially have stories to tell, and if they are not recorded, the history will be lost forever. What better way to make grandmother's day, as she is videotaped talking about and making her favorite spaghetti sauce or apple pie. A written copy of the recipe could also be edited in. Clips of Uncle Joe's birthday party75 is a big one and will be cherished forever. How about a keepsake of getting ready and leaving for the Jr. Prom or Mary's first T-ball game?

I hope Kim's story will give you plenty of ideas on how to use your video camera. Many people, when approached, will say they do their own videos; they may, but they are never edited or placed on a DVD that can be watched.

Still searching, let's look at Smitty. He is a self-designated, car-buying consultant. He helps people find the perfect used car. He will meet with his client and compile a profile of what they are looking for and about how much they are willing to pay for the car. Smitty then sets out on the quest to make a happy client. It is good to have a good relationship with many car dealers and a fair knowledge of automobiles. In our fast-moving society, most people don't want to spend days on days going from dealer to dealer. Smitty advises being careful when dealing with individuals that are selling one car, but if you know your cars, go through your checklist and you can make a happy buyer. You can also pick up an extra buck or two by working with credit unions or banks to help with financing.

Many people and businesses need extra help but don't want to hire someone full time. Instead, they use a virtual assistant – Janice, based at home, is a virtual assistant who helps out with phone answering, correspondence, research – almost anything that an in-person assistant would do. Because she works from home, all she needs is a computer, printer and a phone. To attract clients, she started a website, placed ads in local papers and even went door to door. Some virtual assistants work in a niche areas, such as funeral concierge, virtual assistants who handle all the legal and administrative tasks involved in funeral arranging; or virtual dating assistants, who organize and sift through online dating sites to find the perfect match for people with no time.

Dear Valued Reader:

As you search for your part-time-income venture, please don't look so far off into the distance that you overlook you interests and the activities you enjoy and are good at. Whatever you do with your venture, keeping it part-time or developing it into a full-time business, make sure it is pleasurable for you.

Be true to your dreams, and keep them alive. Never let anyone change your mind about what you feel you can achieve. Always believe in yourself.

I believe in you. I want to tell you that I believe in you I believe in your mind and all the dreams, intelligence, and determination within you. You can accomplish anything. You have so much open to you, so please don't give up on what you want from life, or from yourself. Please don't put away the dreams inside of you. You have the power to make them real. You have the power to make yourself exactly what you want to be. Believe in yourself the way I do, and nothing will be beyond your reach.

Don't get that feeling that your life is a movie that you're watching, instead of starring in. Enjoy life; this is not a dress rehearsal.

Remember the buck starts here.

Jerry Scicchitano

Sign up for my blog @
@ www.PartTimeIncomeEnterprise.com.

Scan this barcode with your
smart phone and it will
take you to Jerry's web site
www.parttimeincomeenterprise.com

ABOUT THE AUTHOR

 **Jerry Scicchitano** has over thirty years of educational experience as an author and owner of many successful part-time income enterprises. Over the past several years through his writings and seminars Jerry has been helping hundreds of people find the extra-income activity that is right for them. They found that by working only a few extra hours a week, turning their spare time and weekends into wealth and security, enabled them to achieve financial freedom through their own part-time income-producing ventures.

The thrill of developing a part-time business is a dream of many people. Although many people are looking for inspiration and direction, they don't know what they want to do or how to go about doing it.

Jerry has the ability to inspire people of all ages to look inside themselves and discover their own money-earning potential and to put it to work for their special benefit. His high level of enthusiasm will keep you motivated to succeed in your second-income ventures. He will show you how to turn every minute of your free time into money with proven examples of how others have put it to work. His proven leadership is just what you need to earn that extra income you and your family are looking for.

Now it's your turn.

For information on local seminars in your area, or to schedule one for your group, contact:

Jerry Scicchitano,

14104 Warwick Blvd #2341,

Newport News VA 23609

E-mail: PartTimeIncomeEnterprise@gmail.com.

Phone (757) 810-0208

Or visit his web page @ www.PartTimeIncomeEnterprise.com.

 Scan this barcode with your smart phone and it will take you to Jerry's web site www.parttimeincomeenterprise.com

Once again thank you for buying my book and good luck on earning the extra money you need to live the life style you and your family deserves.

CPSIA information can be obtained at www.ICGtesting.com
Printed in the USA
BVOW071052090513

320317BV00002B/102/P